# Legendary Love Stories

# Legendary Love Stories

Peter Guttmacher

MetroBooks

# MetroBooks

An Imprint of Friedman/Fairfax Publishers

© 1997 by Michael Friedman Publishing Group, Inc.

Library of Congress Cataloging-in-Publication Data

Guttmacher, Peter.
    Legendary love stories / Peter Guttmacher.
          p.  cm.
    Includes bibliographical references and index.
    ISBN 1-56799-489-X
    1. Love in motion pictures.     I. Title.
  PN1995.9.L6G88  1997
  791.43′6543—dc21           97-7237

Editor: Tony Burgess
Art Director: Jeff Batzli
Designer: Andrea Karman and Jan Melchior
Photography Editors: Christopher C. Bain and Amy Talluto
Production Manager: Jeanne Hutter

Color separations by Bright Arts Graphics (S) Pte Ltd
Printed in China by Leefung

1 3 5 7 9 10 8 6 4 2

For bulk purchases and special sales, please contact:
Friedman / Fairfax Publishers
Attention: Sales Department
15 West 26th Street
New York, NY 10010
212/685-6610 FAX 212/685-1307

Visit our website:
http://www.metrobooks.com

## ACKNOWLEDGMENTS

*Hello there, young lovers, you're under arrest... The author would like to thank his dashing editor, Tony Burgess, the dreamy staff at the Academy of Motion Picture Arts and Sciences' Center for Motion Picture Study, and his own true sweetheart, Robin Rose. This labor of love is dedicated to lovers in labor, Tom and Carol...and their little love bundle to come.*

# CONTENTS

# INTRODUCTION

*I*f love and sex and all that come from them weren't mankind's whole reason for being, movies might not even exist and life would just be an incredibly long documentary.

So, who watches movies? Almost everybody. If some berserk university professor asked you to divide movie-watching humanity into two groups that transcended gender, race, creed, and economic status, what would you come up with? The answer is simple: single people and people in relationships. If the pestering prof's next query was what kind of videos do most couples bring home on a Saturday night (when the man doesn't coerce his mate into watching action/adventure) to unwind with, escape with, feel cozy with, or get turned on by, what would you say? How about the single folk? What do most have on their minds (spiritually and carnally) a vast majority of the time? What do they look to at up to $9 a pop to keep up their courage for their quest? If you answered love stories, go to the head of the class.

Love stories. Some of us live for them; some of us try to live up to them; some of us just live them (who are we kidding?). Nothing is more imbued with the magic that movies have to give than a great love story. Little on the big screen can be as elating, depressing, or arousing (depending on the film and your mood). When the special effects du jour cease to titillate, when the car chases are just so much burning rubber, when the action heroes start to blur into each other's biceps, we return to what movies, at their best, have always been all about—story, acting, and heart. These movies may be sappy, savage, sexy, sick, scandalous, or insurrectionist, but they get to the core of what interests us the most—human relationships.

On a canvas that big there's always been ample room for filmic artists to paint epics as sweepingly diverse as Alfonso Arau's *Like Water for Chocolate* (1992) and Chen Kaige's *Farewell, My Concubine* (1993), homages as hiply homespun as Spike Lee's

*She's Gotta Have It* (1986) or Rob Reiner's *When Harry Met Sally...* (1989), and portraits as unblinkingly intimate as Ingmar Bergman's *Scenes from a Marriage* (1973) or Mike Figgis' *Leaving Las Vegas* (1995).

Like the history books you always wish you'd been given in school, legendary love stories are juicy, true chronicles of their age. They tell volumes about the cherished beliefs and lofty ideals that make up a generation, just as the lifestyles of their stars often tell another, darker, more dysfunctional story. Whether lensed in the Roaring Twenties, the madcap Depression thirties, the sacrificial forties, the staid fifties, the revolutionary sixties, the me-oriented seventies, the idealless eighties, or the new nineties, the journeys that each of these films (sleeper and blockbuster alike) makes from conception to projection is the story of the way we live and love (or would like to think we do).

*Legendary Love Stories* is your invitation to a uniquely entertaining, informative, and up-to-date look at the dream factory, not only in Hollywood, but across the globe. We'll savor the performances that so often made movie stars out of actors, from Louise Brooks to Marlon Brando to Billy Crystal. We'll go behind the scenes to get the inside scoop about the writing, casting, and shooting of some of your favorite flicks (from fluff to fury) and turn you on to other gems that might have come and gone before you could catch them.

Our somewhat insubordinate investigations will run the gamut from insults exchanged between sex symbols; documented techniques for ducking censorship; late-breaking leaks about scandalous movie-star behavior; challenges to untangle mismatched couples of the screen and identify immortal lines of romantic dialogue; precious celebrity pearls on love, marriage, and divorce; and directors' secrets for getting screen lovers in the mood. Surprises will be many, disappointments will be few, and no prisoners will be taken.

So, put your heart on your sleeve, keep your wits sharp and your eyes open, and let us go where so very many have gone before...but never like this.

**OPPOSITE: Ill-fated lovers Romeo (Leonard Whiting) and Juliet (Olivia Hussey) enjoy their brief moment in the sun before tragedy overtakes them in Franco Zefferelli's 1968 film version.**

# Chapter One

# HAPPILY EVER AFTER, OR GET OUT YOUR POPCORN

*Love is sweeping the country.*
*Waves are hugging the shore.*
*All the sexes from Maine to Texas have never seen such love before.*
*See them billing and cooing, like the birdies above,*
*    each girl and boy alike, sharing joy alike,*
*    feels a passion'll soon be national.*
*Love is sweeping the country, there's never been so much love.*

—from "Love Is Sweeping the Country" by George and Ira Gershwin

So many men, so little time, muses heiress/goddess Tracy Lord (Katharine Hepburn) as ex-husband C. Dexter Haven (Cary Grant), lover Mike Connor (Jimmy Stewart), and fiancé George Kitteridge (John Howard) hang on her every word in **The Philadelphia Story** *(1940).*

# Silent Kisses

A boy. A girl. A happy ending. Maybe even a sunset for them to walk into together. Is that too much to ask? Sometimes there is no greater recipe for losing the blues. After all the film scholars have had to say about montage, religious symbolism, and plot structure, it's really how the story comes out in the end that counts. When love triumphs with a minimum of muss, fuss, and heartbreak, we love to watch. So what if it isn't exactly like real life? It's better than the real thing. It's perfect. It's…happily ever after.

When projected film made its American debut at Koster & Bial's Music Hall in New York on April 26, 1896, Thomas Edison's Vitascope Company included one surefire crowd pleaser. Second in popularity only to dramatic footage of waves crashing along the British coast (a romantic metaphor, itself) was a smoochy little number called *The May Irwin Kiss*. In close-up, two distinctly middle-aged thespians, May Irwin and a mustachioed John Rice, replicated their meeting-of-the-mouths from the theatrical hit *The Widow Jones*. Audiences giggled, cooed, and came back for a second viewing.

And why not? It had been a rough century. The American Civil War, the Franco-Prussian War, the Russo-Turkish War, the Sino-Japanese War, the British-Zulu War, the Chicago Fire, the Little Bighorn, Wounded Knee, Jack the Ripper, Armenian massacres, and the assassination of two American presidents had all been squeezed into a little more than three decades.

To escape the stress of it all, nineteenth-century audiences had consistently flocked to romantic melodramas, which, introduced in England by 1802, had become a staple of American theater with classics like *Under the Gaslight* (1867). The lighter side of love had to settle for making itself known through musicals, owing much to the sentiment and romantic European settings of operettas. Blithely witty, romantic comedies the likes of Oscar Wilde's *The Importance of Being Earnest* (1895) also sweetened the theatrical pot with a dash of urbane sophistication.

Swinging into the end of the century, popular stage entertainment luckily swung away from melodrama to swashbuckling adventure and passionate romance with matinee idols, both imported and domestic. Plays with titles like *A Parisian Romance* and *A Russian Honeymoon* were the hits of 1883. The

## On an Up Note: Vive L'amour

*There are as many views on love as there are stars in the firmament. Let's see what strange light these stars have shed on the positive side of love.*

*I can't come up with words poetic enough to describe her. She had a very strong aura. She struck me as being stunning. Not pretty, but very beautiful in a powerful way. Deep class.*

—Jack Nicholson on meeting Angelica Huston

*Love between two people is wonderful—if you can get between the right two people.*

—Woody Allen

*It's a grand idea to marry three or four times, have lots of children and remain friendly all around. It's a vitalizing, typically American plan. I endorse it without a quibble or qualm. My wives are lovely, my children adorable. I count myself a very lucky man.*

—John Barrymore

*I saw your test [for* To Have and Have Not*]. We're going to have a lot of fun together.*

—Humphrey Bogart upon his introduction to Lauren Bacall

*Marriage requires a special talent, like acting, like writing. I haven't got that talent, so I don't marry. And monogamy requires genius.*

—Warren Beatty

*I can get a divorce whenever I want to. But my wife and Kate [Hepburn] like things just as they are.*

—Spencer Tracy to Joan Fontaine

*I have a love interest in every one of my films—a gun.*

—Arnold Schwarzenegger

Love was slowly sweeping the country, but before it could really clean up at the cinema, the movies themselves had to gain a little in length and loosen up a bit. A 5¢ ticket to an early nickelodeon usually got you an evening of six one-reel films, each lasting about ten to fifteen minutes and often including an adventure, a comedy, a chase, and a melodrama. Visual stimulus was the name of the game for early audiences of working-class and immigrant spectators. Literacy couldn't be counted on, so subtitled stories weren't as important as spectacle.

Only with Thomas Edison and the Motion Picture Patents Company's greedy move in 1907 to distribute films at a higher price to a more literate and moneyed audience did the narrative film and love story begin to bloom in earnest. Thanks in large part to the prolific pioneering of director David Wark "D. W." Griffith from 1910 to 1920, storytelling on film was no longer limited to flat recordings of stage melodramas, but included a dazzling array of close-ups, medium shots, pans, and intercutting between two scenes, as well as a fresh focus on character.

Nevertheless, most of the tales remained melodramatic. Griffith occasionally lightened up with romantic one-reel comedies like *The New York Hat* (1912), whose script was based on a freelance submission by teenage writer Anita Loos (who, decades later, would write the stage play for *Gigi*). Sarah Bernhardt's romantic, four-reel (one hour of story) French production *Les Amours de la Reine Elizabeth* (1912) spurred American filmmakers to create longer and more romantic films. Director Maurice Tourneur romanced audiences even further with *The Wishing Ring* (1914) and its beautiful wedding finale with its two romantic leads, Vivian Martin and Alec B. Francis.

Slowly the star system helped romance in movies, too. Hollywood's first real movie star, America's sweetheart, Mary Pickford (who portrayed a twelve-year-old when she was twenty-seven), while a tad too young for screen romance herself, introduced the Gish sisters (Lillian and Dorothy) to Griffith. Lillian, whose combined fragile exterior and inner strength made her the "First Lady of the Silent Screen," was soon the reigning melodramatic heroine. And though she may have gotten a happy ending in Griffith's tale of unrequited love finally requited, *True Heart Susie* (1919), her romantic roles weren't conducive to much in the way of fun.

After all, the Victorian era was just a stone's throw behind—bubbly, happy endings and love without hard-won lessons smacked of loose living. The fairer sex was meant to be either serious and pure or desirable and dirty. And unless the actresses were willing to roughhouse it in madcap, slapstick comedies the way troopers like Mabel Norman did, breezy screen time just wasn't in the picture.

dashing Maurice Barrymore (ancestor of Drew), the multifaceted Richard Mansfield, and the stately Anglo import Henry Irving all swooned the ladies. Likewise, whether it was Italy's Eleanor Duse as Camille, France's Sarah Bernhardt as Cleopatra, America's Maude Adams as Juliet, British heartthrob Lily Langtry, or stateside chanteuse Lillian Russell in just about anything, gentlemen wanted more l'amour (remember, professional football had only been in progress since 1895 and television hadn't been invented yet).

*OPPOSITE: Humphrey Bogart and Lauren Bacall had it sweet despite a decade or two of age difference. TOP: Angelica Huston and Jack Nicholson were quite an item for quite a while. BOTTOM: But Annette Bening and Warren Beatty had more than a Love Affair...if less than a great movie.*

# Walking Into the Sunrise

*P*erhaps the perfect example of having to wade through the wages of sin to find a nice happy ending to a love story was a visually stunning piece of melodrama that many cite as the very culmination of the silent cinema. Its ending may be as pure and heartfelt as the dawn, but oh, what a night of storm and suffering had to be endured for *Sunrise: A Tale of Two Humans* (1927).

*Sunrise's* director, the great F. W. Murnau, had been the toast of the precocious German cinema, which was far outclassing Hollywood in the early twenties. Such visually thrilling, atmospheric classics as *Nosferatu* (1922), the unauthorized film adaptation of Bram Stoker's novel *Dracula*, and *The Last Laugh* (1924), the surprisingly tragic story of a stuffy hotel doorman who ends up a washroom attendant, had made Murnau a legend. Hollywood, with its "If you can't beat 'em, buy 'em" mentality, gave Murnau both a four-year, four-picture contract —$125,000 for his first to $200,000 for his last—and carte blanche on a story that was written and designed in Berlin, but cast and shot on the lot of Fox Studios in the good old U.S.A.

Released the same year as the first talkie, *The Jazz Singer* (1927), *Sunrise* revolves around a lumbering hulk of a farmer (George O'Brien), his blonde-headed angel of a wife (Janet Gaynor), and the dark and lithesome vamp vacationing from the city (Margaret Livingston) who almost steals his soul. During the farmer's sexually ecstatic moonlit trysts with the vamp (she always signals them by whistling just outside his cottage), she convinces him to drown his wife in a "boating accident" and then come to the city. He almost does it, too, having enticed his wife on a ride across the lake to the city for a holiday and having hidden aboard some bulrushes picked by his lover to assure his own floatation.

When push literally comes to shove, he can't go through with it. As they reach the far shore, the sobbing, shattered wife runs for her life, with her now-repentant husband in hot pursuit on the trolley into the city. It's only when she seeks sanctuary in a church during a beautiful wedding that they're both thunderstruck and reconnected to the power of their own love. Then, through a day filled with rekindled love, the couple frolics in the big city like kids in a candy store. He gets spruced up (while a stranger flirting with his wife shows him how desirable she is) and they buy flowers, stiffly pose for a portrait photographer (who instead snaps one of their fervent clinches when they think he's changing film), play in an amusement park, rescue a runaway pig, demonstrate country

**RIGHT: Silent romance at its very best. Faithless husband George O'Brien is harboring evil thoughts about his innocent peasant wife, Janet Gaynor, but will love triumph over lust by Sunrise (1927)?**

dancing to wild applause, and are subsequently allowed to get tipsy in a fancy restaurant.

On their romantic sail back through the moonlight, tragedy strikes in the form of a torrential windstorm and then thunderstorm. You guessed it—they are swept overboard, but not before he gives her the bulrushes. He washes up on shore alone and calls out a frantic search of villagers over the black water, to no avail. Sobbing at his wife's empty bed, he hears the whistle of you-know-who and, well…let's just say that right triumphs in all kinds of ways.

A simple story, with bravura acting and cinematography, sets, and lighting lush enough to drown in—the happy ending (which shall remain nameless) wasn't always so happy. Hermann Suderman's story "Excursion to Tilsit" made O'Brien's character much more of a brute and had things end badly for him. Both Murnau and screenwriter Carl Mayer knew that wouldn't wash in Hollywood, so they made it upbeat and put in twice as many title cards as they would have for the more visually-minded German audiences. In return, William Fox, the owner of Fox Studios, did something almost unheard of: he left Murnau completely alone with unlimited funds. The production accountant went to New York for nine months to save his sanity. Only Murnau, his cinematographers, Karl Struss and Charles Rosher, and his editor, Katherine Hilliker, would see a frame of it before completion.

What a movie they made! With the months of planning in Berlin that yielded plaster models and more than two hundred sketches from art director Rochus Gliese, Struss and Rosher were able to plan their fantastic camera work and lighting down to a T. *Sunrise* was filled with sensual obscurities. From the cigarette smoke that curls around the vamp's scantily-clad body to the ominous smoke billowing from a bonfire on a passing barge to marsh mists and the moon shrouded in fog, the film was, in the words of contemporary Oscar-winning cinematographer Nestor Alemendros, "so atmospheric, you could almost touch the air and smell it." And in the time before optical printers, every special effect was done in the camera.

Before Orson Welles or Robert Altman ever dazzled audiences with depth of focus and long tracking shots, Murnau was snaking the camera through fen and thicket as he followed the heavy-breathing, heavy-stepping George O'Brien stalking across the moonlit

marsh to meet his writhing temptress. To do this, the director had to build a complex system of overhead rails on which the camera was to glide over the Fox set.

Expressionistic set devices, which Murnau had learned so well studying under the great German theater director Max Reinhardt, filled the movie. Tilted walls, raked ceilings and floors, and a multitude of glass and mirrored surfaces made "the city" a gleaming, dangerous place that dwarfed its inhabitants. Indeed, crowds of hundreds of dwarves were used in backgrounds to force perspective even further. When Murnau saw a tree he liked as he and his crew were laying trolley tracks by Lake Arrowhead, California, he had it dug up and transplanted to the Fox set. When blazing lights withered the leaves, he hired a crew of three hundred laborers to glue substitutes on. When the lights withered the fakes as well, a second batch of better leaves was added.

The amazing thing is that none of these pyrotechnics overpowered the love story. Critics forecast that Murnau, a known homosexual, would be incapable of crafting a convincing heterosexual love story. How wrong they were. O'Brien's transition from a lustful Frankenstein to a tender husband is a sight to behold. As for the glamorous Janet Gaynor, sticking a homely blonde wig on her tresses and frumping her up was the best thing anyone ever did for her. Her soul shines through like a beacon. As Murnau said, "I wished Janet Gaynor to play not Janet Gaynor, the screen beauty, but a poor, stupid, peasant girl. I had to submerge her physical beauty to emphasize the beauty of her heart."

At the very first Academy Awards, in 1927, Gaynor, Struss, and Rosher all garnered Oscars for their outstanding work. But the film cost a fortune, so from then on the Fox brass was all over Murnau's movies and their budgets. As a result, the silent-story teller would break his contract with Fox and go on to co-direct the South Seas docudrama *Tabu* (1931), only to be killed in a car crash the week before its opening.

*One would hesitate to call any film the finest of its era, though as a climax to the art of the silent film, one could certainly defend that statement if it were applied to Sunrise [1927]. But quite certainly, it is a textbook illustration not only of what the silent film could achieve despite the lack of dialogue, but on the contrary, what it could achieve because of it.*

**—William K. Everson from *Romance in the Film***

# THOROUGHLY MODERN MILLIE AND THE LUBITSCH TOUCH

*L*uckily, happy endings didn't forever hinge on redemption or pit the chaste against the impure. When the twenties roared in, Prohibition, bathtub gin, a fat and happy postwar economy, the Charleston, and, most important, women's suffrage did more than change society. Having won the right to vote in 1920, women got a little room to move on the silver screen and happy endings got a little more complex. More empowered, equal to their mates, women took the screen by storm.

Names like Gloria Swanson, Vilma Banky, and Dolores Costello were soon giving matinee idols like John Gilbert and Rudolf Valentino a run for their box-office money. With a rejection of grandma Victoria, the life-loving flapper was queen. Up rocketed frothy film star Constance Talmadge, who was so popular as the tomboy in D.W. Griffith's Babylonian epic, *Intolerance* (1916), that he had it rereleased in 1919 to give her a new, happy ending. Talmadge tickled audiences in silence in *The Virtuous Vamp* (1919), *Polly of the Follies* (1922), and *Her Naughty Romance* (1924).

On a less wholesome but still upbeat note, Clara Bow—an emancipated woman, a boss-chasing bombshell, and the "It Girl"—wowed her audiences in steamy romances like *Man Trap* (1926). Just as desirable was Warsaw émigré Pola Negri, Hollywood's first imported star (at $3,000 a week), who would list no less than Charlie Chaplin, Rudolf Valentino, and (rumor had it) Adolf Hitler as her paramours. On the export was the fiery, raven-haired, American actress Louise Brooks, who became a legendary temptress and archetypal flapper in Germany thanks to G.W. Pabst's *Pandora's Box* (1928). Pabst also employed a certain Swedish actress, Greta Gustafson, who would dazzle Hollywood under the imported moniker of Greta Garbo.

These women wielded power. Screenwriter Jeanie Macpherson had already penned many of Cecil B. DeMille's first films between 1914 and 1930. Director Lois Weber lensed eleven social-problem films for her own production company between 1917 and 1921 and six more for other studios. Mary Pickford saw to it that Frances Marion wrote the star vehicle *Lovelight* (1923) for her, as well as eight other films. Pickford, who in 1919 along with Charlie Chaplin, D.W. Griffith, and swashbuckling hubby Douglas Fairbanks, had formed the first powerful independent film company in Hollywood, United Artists, struck gold for romance when she lured another

German director over to direct her in a more mature venue called *Rosita* (1923).

Ernst Lubitsch was a short, sassy, cigar-chomping marvel. This infectiously enthusiastic man, who later made Garbo laugh in *Ninotchka* (1939) and whose *To Be or Not to Be* (1942) managed to make a Polish Shakespearean troupe doing *Hamlet* in Nazi Germany funny during wartime, could seemingly do anything. One of the few Hollywood legends in his own time, he was such a mensch that after insisting on real snow for his Jimmy Stewart/Margaret O'Sullivan combative store clerk romance, *The Shop Around the Corner* (1940), he outfitted his cast and crew with forty-three pairs of galoshes to ward off any colds.

In the early thirties, Lubitsch turned out what many consider the very best of all his love stories. Lubitsch himself admitted, "As for pure style I think I have done nothing better or as good." If you like sexual allusion cloaked by sparkling banter, as well as an idyllic world where everyone is as urbane as they are irresistible, look no further.

From its very first shot, you know *Trouble in Paradise* (1932) will be deliciously lacking in conventionality. Set in Venice, a less-inspired film would have established an atmosphere of romance

**ABOVE: With dialogue that sparkled with wit and sophisticated repartée, Cary Grant and Grace Kelly stole each other's hearts in To Catch a Thief (1955).**
**RIGHT: Actresses like Louise Brooks, here in G. W. Pabst's German-made Pandora's Box (1928), proved to Hollywood that women could exude as much power and potency as men on the screen...though this heroine is eventually murdered for her man-hungry ways.**

with a long shot of the canal-filled city fading into a particularly picturesque street, fading to a house, fading to a window out of which beautiful opera is being sung. Lubitsch asked screenwriter Samson Raphaelson, "How do we do that without doing that?" The answer was beautiful singing to be romantically tracked down to an operatic garbage collector. So begins a story of la crème and la scum.

As Gaston and Lily, a coolly continental Herbert Marshall and an electric Miriam Hopkins are a couple of crooks who meet and fall in love with stealing from each other in Venice, where Gaston has just fleeced a fellow guest while masquerading as a hotel doctor. When he snags a bag at the opera and discovers it belongs to the perfume heiress Mariette Colet (Kay Francis), he returns it for a

ABOVE: Only the great and crafty Lubitsch could get away with having his **Trouble in Paradise (1932)** hero Gaston (Herbert Marshall) dallying with both perfume heiress Mariette (Kay Francis on the left) and fellow felon Lily (Miriam Hopkins) in the same movie. RIGHT: Tripping the light fantastically, Fred Astaire, Ginger Rogers, and a whole lotta ostrich feathers go dancing cheek-to-cheek in their unforgettable **Top Hat (1935)**.

hefty reward and so charms her that he lands a job as her personal secretary. He wangles Lily onto the staff and together they plan to rob Mariette blind.

The problem is that the beautiful heiress is just as suave and seductive as either of her assailants (though Miriam Hopkins' chair did have to be nailed to the set to keep her from swiveling to upstage Francis) and Gaston soon finds himself falling for both his boss and the perfume business. Will he go straight or crooked? Will he love high or low? How is a happy ending possible? It's quite a chase to get there and interesting to note that Marshall managed affairs with Hopkins, Francis, and Gloria Swanson dur-

ing the filming period. Scandalous? Not to Lubitsch, whose next film, *Design For Living* (1933), would be about a very contented ménage à trois.

# GIVE ME FANTASY OR GIVE ME DEATH

omance's loose-living heyday didn't last long. Boom went the stock market crash of 1929. Boom deepened the Depression throughout the thirties. Boom went the Hollywood Production Code censors of 1935, cleaning up for hard times. With America reeling from hunger and joblessness, flappers flapped to earth and moral complexity wasn't the key to anyone's heart. Fairy-tale romance was much more the order of the day, where sophistication was so godlike that it was hardly sullied by sex. It was provided in spades by Ginger Rogers and Fred Astaire.

Their quintessential vehicle, *Top Hat* (1935), had audiences (to quote Fred himself) "stepping out my dear, to breathe an atmosphere that simply reeks of class." Class it was. In a world of swank evening clothes, exclusive London men's clubs, art deco hotel suites, and flights down to Venice's Lido, American dancing star Jerry Travers (Fred) and feisty fashion model Dale Tremont (Ginger) glide their way through a comedy of mistaken identity (Dale thinks the besmitten Jerry is her best friend's husband), stopping only to verbally skirmish, drink champagne, and dance…dance…dance.

The dance of romance is everywhere. When Jerry's tap dancing (the "No Strings" number) in his producer's (the incomparable Edward Everett Horton) deluxe London apartment disturbs Dale's slumber in the apartment below, he sprinkles sand on his floor from a nearby ashtray and soft-shoes her to sleep again. He tap dances over her again while hijacking her hansom cab. When they find themselves caught by a thundershower in a park's gazebo (with Fred in a casual suit and Ginger in riding attire), a spirited dance competition quickly becomes a whirling, swirling, lightning, brightening love ritual.

Rogers was originally partnered with the Broadway star only when his previous leading lady, the ballet-trained Dorothy Jordan, quit the biz to marry RKO's head of production. In stepped Ginger and off they went *Flying Down to Rio* (1933). They may have been secondary characters (a corny accordionist and a sassy club singer), but when they got the chance to do their version of the Brazilian carioca dance, magic happened.

Thanks to the beautiful duo, the movie made more money than any other RKO picture that year except *Little Women* (not bad for the worst winter of the Depression). And the MGM executive who

allegedly assessed Astaire's first screen test with the pronouncement, "Can't act, can't sing, balding, can dance a little," was off somewhere dining on chapeau.

This romance had its price. Astaire had spent years partnered onstage with his sister, Adele, but what he craved was solo stardom. He wrote to his agent, Leland Hayward, "I don't mind making another picture with her [Rogers], but as for this team idea, it's out! I've just managed to live down one partnership and I don't want to be bothered with any more." But their future pairing was inevitable. Rogers' open earthiness, hard-boiled banter, and classic blonde goddess looks seemed to give frailer, flap-eared Fred the sex appeal he needed (though they never actually kissed until their next-to-last film together, *The Story of Vernon & Irene Castle*, 1939). In turn, he made her a class act when they danced, proving to all that you don't need to leave the ballroom floor to make love.

Travers was Astaire's favorite role and *Top Hat* was the first RKO vehicle written especially for the duo. One famous dance, "Top Hat, White Tie, and Tails," came to the film from Astaire's 1930 Ziegfeld show, *Smiles*. The inspiration for the stage number came in the middle of the night. "I woke suddenly," Astaire fondly recalled, "visualizing a row of top-hatted men. I saw myself shooting them down, one by one, with my walking stick, while I simulated the sound of a machine gun with my tapping feet. I was so stirred by the possibilities of this number that I jumped out of bed, grabbed a handy umbrella and started practicing it. Soon my sister, Adele, called from the next room of our apartment to ask what in the world I was doing." The day it was shot for the film, fellow hoofer

> Feathers—I hate feathers.
> And I hate them so that I can hardly speak,
> And I never find the happiness I seek
> With those chicken feathers dancing cheek to cheek.
>
> —Fred Astaire's commentary after the infamous ostrich incident during the filming of *Top Hat* (1935)

Jimmy Cagney strolled over to watch and informed Astaire after a few tries, "Don't shoot it again, kid, you got it on the second take." He had.

Indeed, Astaire was a perfectionist, working tirelessly on steps with his own choreographer, Hermes Pan. Pan then taught the steps to Rogers, and Rogers and Astaire would practice and film for hours and hours until it had that effortless look. In *Swing Time* (1936) they filmed the finale for "Never Gonna Dance" so many times (forty-seven, to be exact) that Ginger's bleeding feet staining her slippers stopped the shooting.

Astaire's future dance partner Leslie Caron remembered that even during breaks he was always "doodling." It wasn't unusual coming back from a breath of fresh air to find him trying out a piece of choreography with a coatrack. His perfectionism certainly paid off in *Top Hat*'s fabled nightclub number, "Cheek to Cheek," but not before a mishap that almost ended his partnership with Rogers.

Rogers was decked out in a slinky blue satin gown covered with willowy, undulating ostrich feathers. Unfortunately, she had rehearsed in something else and her plumage was less than secure. On their first take dancing the number, so many loose feathers flew around the dancers (up Astaire's nose and in his eyes) that in Astaire's words it was "as if a chicken had been attacked by a coyote." Astaire was furious and, though the film's seamstress later sewed each feather on individually, you can still see the odd plume float by in the final product.

The dream team patched things up—Rogers retained the nickname "Feathers" and Astaire checked her costumes in the future.

They went on to revolutionize not only dance, but the whole way dance was filmed (now following the whole sweep of the dancer's body instead of focusing on individual parts). They parted in 1939 after nine films. Though they had been a screen marriage made in heaven, Rogers admitted, "When you work with somebody all day long for ten movies, you become good friends, though he was as delighted not to see me at night over dinner as I was." Rogers had her sights on being a serious actress and eventually was, winning the Best Actress Oscar for *Kitty Foyle* (1940) and getting a telegram from her old dance partner that simply read, "Ouch!"

By chance, they reunited after a retired Astaire replaced Gene Kelly to star with Judy Garland in *Easter Parade* (1948) and Rogers was brought in to replace the ailing Garland in *The Barkleys of Broadway* (1949). The world was a safer place by then, and happy endings were a whole new ball game, but as Hermes Pan noted, "There was something when Fred and Ginger danced together that was magic." There would never be another pair like them.

*ABOVE: Even Federico Fellini tried his continental hand at dance and romance with his own idol, Marcello Mastroianni, and Giulietta Masina in the satirical* Ginger and Fred *(1986). OPPOSITE: She may not have been a pussycat to the press, but Katharine Hepburn proved she could do screwball, romantic comedy as she hunts for a loose leopard with paleontologist Cary Grant in* Bringing Up Baby *(1938).*

# THE ANTIDOTE, OR KATE'S FALL TO GRACE

The early forties showed that happy endings could be earned without searing your soul in melodrama hell, frolicking in frothy sin, or dancing the night away without a thought in your head. Living through a little good-natured purgatory would do just fine. With the Great Depression a not-so-distant memory and upheaval in Europe getting stronger by the day, even the romantic comedies of Frank Capra, Howard Hawks, Gregory LaCava, and Preston Sturges were sometimes stinging sociopolitical lessons in love. Good romance taught its protagonists something about themselves, especially if they were rich.

In 1940, before Katharine Hepburn was a thinking man's love goddess, she was in deep trouble. Before winning her four (count 'em, four—an unbeaten record) Oscars, conducting a lifelong love affair and screen partnership with Spencer Tracy from *Woman of the Year* (1942) to *Guess Who's Coming to Dinner* (1967), chugging upstream into adventure with Bogey in *The African Queen* (1951), falling for Rossano Brazzi in *Summertime* (1955), holding out against Burt Lancaster in *The Rainmaker* (1956), wrangling with Peter O'Toole in *The Lion in Winter* (1968), courting Laurence Olivier in *Love Among the Ruins* (1975), being courted by John Wayne in *Rooster Cogburn* (1975), nestling with Henry Fonda in *On Golden Pond* (1981), and chaperoning Warren Beatty and Annette Bening in *Love Affair* (1994), Hepburn had to save a sinking career with just such a light-hearted romance—one of the wittiest ever lensed, *The Philadelphia Story* (1940).

The charismatic daughter of a suffragist and a lawyer, and a 1928 graduate of Bryn Mawr, Hepburn was used to success. The Broadway play *The Warrior Husband* (1932) had won her her first contract with RKO. Her own Yankee hardheadedness won her unrivaled terms of script choice and salary for a rookie or a woman. Though she weathered womanizer John Barrymore's advances while playing his devoted daughter in her screen debut, *A Bill of*

> No longer does Miss Hepburn throw temper fits on the lot, act uppish with fans, sass traffic cops, and dress like a ragamuffin while driving a Hispano-Suiza. Older and wiser, she's behaving admirably. She is still colorful and independent but not making a colossal pose of it.
>
> —*Look* magazine, December 31, 1940

> Show me an actress who isn't a personality and you'll show me a woman who isn't a star.
>
> —Katharine Hepburn

*Divorcement* (1932), and won his friendship in the process (though some say she told Barrymore after filming, "Thank God this is over. Now I don't have to act with you anymore," to which he responded, "My dear, I wasn't aware that you ever had."), the rest of Hollywood was less impressed by her refusal to play the studio game like a good little starlet.

She wouldn't pose for pinup pictures. She didn't wear makeup. She wouldn't give autographs or grant interviews. What few photo opportunities she had often found her in slacks. She fought with directors. Her passionate perfectionism may have won her an Oscar for her work in *Morning Glory* (1933), but her heady ways, less-than-delicate voice (Tallulah Bankhead once described it as sounding like nickels dropping into a slot), and often questionable choice of scripts and roles (playing an androgynous lass a little too well in *Sylvia Scarlett*, 1935) sunk her slowly all through the thirties.

*Mary of Scotland* (1936) was a snooze. Ginger Rogers stole her thunder as the wide-eyed ingenue in *Stage Door* (1937). And even her heroic leap into full-blown screwball comedy with Cary Grant in Howard Hawks' rapid-fire masterpiece *Bringing Up Baby* (1938) didn't keep the press from dubbing her "Katharine of Arrogance." Nor did it stop the powerful Independent Theater Owners' Association from adding her to their published list of box-office poison (stars with huge salaries who were a bust with moviegoers).

Hepburn left the Hollywood loop to escape her downward spiral. The Theater Guild talked the veteran stage actress into taking *Jane Eyre* on tour. It closed during out-of-town tryouts. Fortune smiled, however, when playwright Philip Barry wrote her the role of a lifetime (or one of them, in Hepburn's case). He had loved her as a rugged individualist paired with Cary Grant in George Cukor's 1938 film adaptation of his own *Holiday*. He offered to write her a romantic comedy (with her input) about a bright, beautiful, rich, arrogant, unattainable, WASPy ice princess named Tracy Lord and her long road to humanization (something many agreed Hepburn needed herself). *The Philadelphia Story* was born.

The stage and subsequent film role was based not on Hepburn, but on the rebellious Philadelphia "Main Line" heiress, Helen Hope Montgomery, who had married a classmate of Barry's from Harvard. In rejection of the foibles of both her philandering father and her often drunk ex-husband, the playboy C. K. Dexter Haven, perfectionist Tracy has plans to marry the sensible and safe (if stuffy and social-climbing) George Kitteridge. The problem is that Haven, in a gallant effort to buy off a scandal story about his ex-father-in-law, has agreed to sneak two *Spy* magazine reporters (Mike Connor, who has nothing but contempt for the upper class, and his wisecracking photographer fiancée, Liz Imbrie) into Tracy's wedding party. They get a society scoop and Haven gets a chance to upset his ex's equilibrium. Further complications arise when (1) Tracy finds herself outcast by almost everyone for being too coldly perfect, (2) havoc-wreaking Haven finds he's still in love with Tracy, a.k.a. Red, (3) the unaffected Connor finds himself more and more affected by the transforming Miss Lord, and (4) Tracy realizes she may be in love with Mike or even Dex but certainly not George.

Hepburn liked the part so much that she not only financed one-fourth of the play, but with the help of friend and lover Howard Hughes, she bought the film rights for it, too. The play, of course, was a Broadway hit (with Joseph Cotten as Haven, Van Heflin as Connor, and Shirley Booth as Imbrie), running 416 performances on tour, and when MGM wanted to option it for the screen for Joan Crawford, the studio execs got a little surprise: the film's owner would sell it only if she starred, had approval on the director, and got not one but two box-office antidotes as leading men.

She asked MGM lion Louis B. Mayer for a famed woman's director, her old friend George Cukor. She got him. She asked for no less than Clark Gable and Spencer Tracy. When they weren't interested, Mayer scored Jimmy Stewart and it was up to Hepburn herself to bag old buddy Grant. She offered Grant either role (Haven's mischievous character had been substantially beefed up for the screen by merging it with Tracy's brother, Sandy). Grant yielded, "Look, I will play C. Dexter Haven and I will give you three weeks." For those three weeks he got $150,000, all of which he donated to the Red Cross and British War Relief.

What a cast! What a movie! What truly sparkling dialogue! Tracy's getting cut down to size to reveal the love goddess within is as romantic as it is painfully funny to watch. From the devilishly dizzy, rich-girl parody she performs (aided by her wacky little sister) for the two journalistic invaders to barbed repartee with her ex to successively wounding dressings-down from both Dex and her father to finally letting it all hang out on her drunken marriage-eve with the love-smitten Connor, Hepburn's underplayed journey is a wonder to watch.

Grant's machinations as her adoring nemesis are similarly restrained artistry of the highest degree—so detached, so charming, yet so affecting when he lets into her with lines like, "You'll never be a first-class human being or a first-class woman until you

learn to have some regard for human frailty. It's a pity your own foot can't slip a little, sometimes."

Though Jimmy Stewart held the public captive, in Ernst Lubitsch's words, "by his very lack of a handsome face and suave

manner," his Connor is the perfect balance to Grant's charisma and romantic dynamite. Stewart was less than convinced of this during filming. Before the famous moonlight-swim scene, he had begged Cukor not to film close-ups of his

skinny frame, claiming, "If I appear in a bathing suit I know it's the end of my career and also the end of the motion picture industry."

By the end of the three weeks of filming and the photo-finish wedding ending, the three stars had a lasting friendship and a hit on their hands. Not only did Jimmy Stewart and screenwriter Donald Ogden Stewart walk away with Oscars, *The Philadelphia Story*'s New York run broke *Snow White*'s 1938 box-office record, and three days after *Story* opened, Hepburn won the New York Film Critics Award for best female performance. Bye-bye, strychnine. Her days as box-office poison were gone for good.

This isn't to say that the heady Miss Hepburn was completely reformed. Still, on the first day of filming, she presented a dead skunk in a casket to the script clerk who would catch her line flubs. She also did a little humanizing of her own. Cukor couldn't tolerate distractions and often screamed "QUIET!" when there was the slightest noise during filming. One day Hepburn convinced the stagehands to make as much commotion as possible. After Cukor stalked offstage to control his temper, she led the entire cast and crew way up into the flies above the soundstage. When Cukor returned, to a desolate set, she signaled all seventy people to yell "QUIET!" down at the bewildered director. Lessons in love and commerce aside, there would never be a total taming of this Kate.

# FOR BETTER OR MUCH WORSE!

*Endings don't get happier than wedding bells. But a wedding doesn't ensure happiness. It doesn't even ensure marriage. Let's test your M.Q. (Moviematrimonial Quotient): marry the marriage to the movie.*

## MARRIAGE

1. You'd abandon your wedding plans, too, if it would mean exposing your illegitimate child to the limelight.

2. Here comes the bride (Wynona Ryder). Here comes the ghoul.

3. It's one thing to create life, but to marry it, too? That's questionable taste.

4. Sure she's marryin' Curly, but Judd might have somethin' to say about it.

5. Jane Russell is the other glamour girl getting married at this double wedding.

6. It was a lovely wedding, but now she has to flee the Nazis.

7. Marriage doesn't mean never having to dress in drag for immigration.

8. His bliss at her marriage is only outmatched by his indebtedness.

9. When it comes down to it, she'd rather marry the guy on the bus.

10. He's not quite Cary Grant in The Philadelphia Story (1940), but this wedding's got music.

11. Just because you slept with her mother is no reason not to try to ruin her wedding ceremony.

12. She may have married a wealthy man, but being "Fourth Mistress" isn't enough for a wife this beautiful.

## MOVIE

A: **Tim Curry** in The Rocky Horror Picture Show *(1975)*

B: **Bing Crosby** in High Society *(1956)*

C: **Cary Grant** in I Was a Male War Bride *(1949)*

D: **Spencer Tracy** in The Father of the Bride *(1950)*

E: **Dustin Hoffman** in The Graduate *(1967)*

F: **Marilyn Monroe** in Gentlemen Prefer Blondes *(1953)*

G: **Shirley Jones** in Oklahoma! *(1955)*

H: **Michael Keaton** in Beetlejuice *(1988)*

I: **Gong Li** in Raise the Red Lantern *(1991)*

J: **Claudette Colbert** in It Happened One Night *(1934)*

K: **Bette Davis** in The Old Maid *(1939)*

L: **Julie Andrews** in The Sound of Music *(1965)*

**Answers**

1=K, 2=H, 3=A, 4=G, 5=F, 6=L, 7=C, 8=D, 9=I, 10=B, 11=E, 12=I

**OPPOSITE: Michael Douglas and Annette Bening discover just how difficult it can be to conduct a love affair in the public eye in The American President.**

# THAT'S AMORE

On the whole, love stories in the late eighties were a little more edgy than they had been in the fluffy fifties (exemplified by films like Doris Day and Rock Hudson's squeaky clean *Pillow Talk*, 1959, or Marilyn Monroe, Lauren Bacall, and Betty Grable's kittenish *How to Marry a Millionaire*, 1953). They were a little more settled than the revolutionary sixties (represented by Dustin Hoffman and Katharine Ross's loss of innocence in *The Graduate*, 1967, or Elliot Gould, Dyan Cannon, Robert Culp, and Natalie Wood's experimentation in *Bob & Carol & Ted & Alice*, 1969). They were certainly less bleak than the singles scene of the me-oriented seventies (as seen in John Travolta's gyrations in *Saturday Night Fever*, 1977, and Diane Keaton's self-destructive debauchery in *Looking for Mr. Goodbar*, 1977). They could be as sweetly sentimental as a couple of old coots like Kate Hepburn and Hank Fonda in *On Golden Pond* (1981) or as sinful as the *Fatal Attraction* (1987) between Michael Douglas and Glenn Close. In short, they were as changeable as the moon.

Director Norman Jewison had already had some weird experiences with "la bella luna" by 1987. On his farm his animals would act strangely under the influence of a full moon. He had had to consult a lunar calendar while shooting *The Cincinatti Kid* (1965) because that same influence usually prodded Steve McQueen to "jump on his motorcycle and disappear into the desert to visit an Indian tribe," he recalled.

When "the Bard of the Bronx," his affectionate title for playwright John Patrick Shanley, came to him with a story about a dour, Brooklyn widow, Loretta Castorini, who under the influence of such a moon falls passionately in love with the wrong person, i.e. her fiancé's moody, one-handed baker brother, Ronny Cammareri, Jewison asked him to read the entire play, acting out all the parts.

Shanley performed an entire Italian American ensemble of characters up to their eyeballs in food, opera, romantic entanglements, and yearnings. Loretta's wealthy, plumber father, Cosmo, was having a long-term affair with a very ripe tomato named Mona. Her mother, the long-suffering Rose, in an attempt to figure her husband's infidelity goes afield and almost does her own research with a Casanova college-professor named Perry. Loretta's intended, Johnny, is an overgrown mama's boy, whose sick mother in Sicily is an impediment to their lackluster marriage plans. Her grandfather is driving the whole house crazy with his pack of mangy dogs. Things are a mess and dutifully going to heal bad blood between Johnny and his younger brother (Ronny cut his hand off in a baking accident when Johnny distracted him) leads to the surprise of her life...one which she will fight tooth and nail...love.

It was a done deal. What else could it be with lines like, "Feed one more bite of my food to your dogs, old man, and I'll kick you to death!"? Rounding up Cher for Loretta, Nicolas Cage for Ronny, Danny Aiello for Johnny, Vincent Gardenia for Cosmo, Anita Gillette for Mona, Olympia Dukakis for Rose, John Mahoney for Perry, Feodor Chaliapin for the old man, and Julie Bovasso (John Travolta's mama from *Saturday Night Fever*, 1977) as Aunt Rita, Jewison had a cast to be envied. He saw them musically: "I've always felt this script had an operatic style. I see Loretta, the heroine of the film, as a lyric soprano. Her fiancé, Mr. Johnny, is the baritone; Mr. Johnny's brother, Ronny, is the tenor, and Loretta's father, Cosmo, is the bass".

When his lyric soprano suddenly got a six-week window of availability because of a delay in the filming of *Suspect* (1987), Jewison and longtime producer Patrick Palmer plunged into an unprecedented two weeks of rehearsals before four weeks of filming. To start with, everyone had to be fluent in Brooklyn Italian dialect (even if interiors would be shot in Toronto for financial reasons). Julie Bovasso, acting teacher and recent dialogue coach for *Prizzi's Honor* (1985), was up to the job, but the soprano had qualms. "I was terrified to try it," admits Cher, "so I didn't open my mouth for almost two days." To help her conquer her fear, Jewison had the star also read lines for Dukakis, who was busy across town on Broadway in Mike Nichols' staging of *Social Security*.

The filming for this loony love story was festive, with Jewison occasionally blowing takes because of his off-camera laughter. "Even if we ruined a shot," emphasized the unusually nebbishy Aiello, "you still couldn't wait to do it again because you knew he was so pleased by what you were doing." Indeed, drenched in moonlight, thanks to director of photography David Watkin's 196 fey lights attached to a giant cherry picker left over from the film *Hanover Street* (1976), there is a divine madness that permeates this operatic story.

Loretta's transformation from bleak bookkeeper to radiant moon goddess culminates when the passionate Ronny implores her into attending a performance of *La Boheme* at Lincoln Center. It's a magical moment for the two working class stiffs (especially when Loretta sees her father with his mistress in the next balcony and he her). The actual shooting was more manic than magic. Jewison had only six hours to get his interiors at the Met with three hundred, fancy-dressed extras. Outside, the hubbub of real patrons exiting, New York City traffic, and throngs of spectators and press frenzied to see Cher in the flesh didn't make things any calmer.

Similarly, shooting in a Carroll Gardens, Brooklyn, bakery proved just as "crustily" New York when a customer barged in demanding his baked goods. Jewison explained that they were trying to make a movie, but the patron persisted, "I don't care what you're trying to make, here. I came all the way from Wall Street and I want my bread!" What else could the director do but direct, "All right, Cher, get the man his bread."

Wrapping under a full moon (real this time) on Friday the 13th, the day before Valentine's Day, *Moonstruck* struck the hearts of audiences. Its operatic plot of classic tragedy and earthy, over-the-top ensemble won Oscars for best actress (Cher), best supporting actress (Dukakis), and best original screenplay (Shanley). Proof, if ever it was needed, that crazy doesn't mean you can't have a happy ending.

It's always appealed to me to see people totally transformed in a movie.

—Cher

Roll over Verdi and give Puccini the news: Lusty baker Nicolas Cage and a widowed Cher plan to do a little operatic wooing of their own in Norman Jewison's romance Italian-style, Moonstruck (1987).

# Chapter Two

# SWEET MISERY, OR GET OUT YOUR HANDKERCHIEFS

*O! Here will I set up my everlasting rest,*
*And shake the yoke of inauspicious stars*
*From this world-wearied flesh. Eyes, look your last!*
*Arms, take your last embrace! and lips,*
   *O you the doors of breath, seal with a righteous kiss*
*A dateless bargain with engrossing death.*

**—Romeo in *Romeo and Juliet*, by William Shakespeare**

*Dr. Fry [a biochemist in the psychiatry department at the Saint Paul Ramsey Medical Center in St. Paul, Minnesota] believes that emotional distress produces toxic substances in the body and that crying helps remove them from the system.*

   *"This may be why someone who is sad feels better after having a good cry," he says.*

   *To test his theory, Dr. Fry organized a study to determine whether emotional tears are chemically different from tears produced by an irritant. Volunteers were asked to watch a Hollywood tearjerker and, if they were moved to weep, to catch their tears in a test tube. A few days later, the same people were exposed to fresh-cut onions and again collected their tears.... His finding confirmed research published in 1957 which demonstrated that emotional tears contain more protein.*

**—from *The Complete Guide to Your Emotions and Your Health*, by Emrika Padus**

Of all the gin joints in all the world she had to walk into his. A bowed Bogey, ready to brace his buried heartbreak, and a tenderly tentative Ingrid Bergman seem to tell the whole sad story without even speaking in the unforgettable classic Casablanca (1942).

*S*ometimes things don't work out. Sometimes Cupid's little love tap ends up being one more of "the slings and arrows of outrageous fortune," to quote a very successful writer. Sometimes it's the fatal blow. Just because you love someone doesn't guarantee that you'll live happily ever after, as every star-crossed lover from Romeo to Prince Charles can confirm. In *Gone With the Wind* (1939) Scarlett O'Hara (Vivien Leigh) may have bucked herself up with "Tomorrow is another day," but the unflip, unvarnished truth is that love isn't easy and fortune can conspire to thwart even the most passionate of paramours. Luckily, that suffering is sweet when you're just watching.

There are few movies that have earned such die-hard or emotional fans as tragic love stories. Until the coming of action/adventure, few had earned as much money. From mad organist Lon Chaney's doomed romance with opera singer Mary Philbin in the silent version of *The Phantom of the Opera* (1925) to mad pianist Gary Oldman's (Ludwig van Beethoven) lost cause of love with a mysterious woman (Johanna Ter Steege) in *Immortal Beloved* (1994),

legions of movies have broken our hearts, emptied our pockets, and depleted our supply of tissues.

Just as melodrama had moralistically reigned over turn-of-the-century theater, the movies gave unhappy endings an official home wherein to hang their black hats during the Great Depression—plots referred to as "weepers." A woman who dared to love a married man and paid the penalty. The country girl shunned because of her love child. The good girl who took the fall for her no-good guy and did time for it. The barriers of poverty, religion, race, nationality—suffering was at a surplus during the thirties and every actress worth her salt (from tears, preferably) took the plunge. From the goddess Greta Garbo (*Susan Lenox: Her Fall and Rise*, 1931) to the siren Marlene Dietrich (*Dishonored*, 1931), women leapt at happiness and fell into the abyss.

Even after the Depression, with the wages of sin substantially reduced, screwball comedy on the loose, and a wartime economy making things less desperate for everyone, a whole new impediment to true love called "the greater good" came on the scene with what many people consider the most romantic movie ever made.

**ABOVE: Even squeezing her brains couldn't make Scarlett O'Hara (Vivien Leigh) a better, kinder, or more willing wife for Rhett Butler (Clark Gable) in the classic of mismatched passions,** Gone With the Wind *(1939). RIGHT: Rick (Bogey) and Ilsa's (Bergman) personal problems may not "amount to a hill of beans" but they sure do make a lot of us cry as* Casablanca *(1942) reaches its sacrificial climax.*

# WE'LL ALWAYS HAVE PARIS

*I*n the fall of 1941, the U.S. population was 131,670,000. What American movie-goers spent yearly at the box office was more than six times that figure. With 20,196 movie houses across the country playing the 598 movies released that year at an average admission of just 25¢, attendance was at an all-time high—even with a year-old war brewing in Europe.

Warner Brothers was doing well because of its success in promoting the "talkies." On December 7, Hal B. Wallis, who had rocketed through the studio's ranks from publicity assistant to production supervisor for all filming, was visiting Hungarian-born director Michael Curtiz (born Mikhaly Kertesz) at his ranch for a weekend of skeet shooting—when other shots were fired across the Pacific. Pearl Harbor had been hit with a sneak attack from the Japanese Imperial Air Force.

As President Roosevelt made his famed declaration of war the following day, Warner Brothers reader Stephen Karnot was sifting through some newly purchased scripts and came across a play called *Everybody Comes to Rick's*. It was by a New York high school teacher named Murray Burnett and his writing partner, Joan Allison. Burnett and his wife, who had traveled to Europe in 1938 to help relatives in Antwerp escape the Nazis, had been in Vienna, Austria, when Hitler took power there. The experience had affected them deeply. They stopped in the south of France on their way home and took refuge in a nightclub overlooking the Mediterranean with an international clientele and a black pianist singing in the middle of it all. Burnette simply said to his wife, "What a setting for a play!"

*Everybody Comes to Rick's* became the story of wartime patriotism told through the tragic love triangle of American cynic Rick Blaine, American beauty Lois Meredith (that's right, Lois Meredith), and European freedom fighter Victor Lazlow. It had distinct differences from its film successor. For instance, Lazlow was wanted by the Nazis for a fortune in illegal gold as well as information. Lois wasn't married to Lazlow—shame! But the play's power and romance won it a grudging option from Broadway producers, with the stipulation of much rewriting. When one producer objected to Lois sleeping with Rick for the exit visas (a nonexistent document dreamed up as a plot device by the playwrights), the writers yanked their play and offered it up to Hollywood.

> *Excellent melodrama. Colorful, timely background, tense mood, suspense, psychological and physical conflict, tight plotting, sophisticated hokum. A box-office natural—for Bogart, or Cagney or Raft in out-of-the-usual roles, and perhaps Mary Astor.*
>
> —original *Warner Bros.* reader's report on *Everybody Comes to Rick's*, the play that led to *Casablanca* (1942)

Warner Brothers had paid $20,000 for it, and now that the war was on (for the United States), it became just the message the doctor (a.k.a. Uncle Sam) ordered. Though far from a blood-and-guts film, the bad guys were bad (as only the frosty German former horror star Conrad Veidt could be as the insidious Major Strasser), the good guys were willing to die for liberty, and the tough guy caught in the middle had the potential to become a hero if he had the love of a beautiful woman. Like the United States itself, Rick hedged in his anti-Nazi position until his own personal Pearl Harbor (the return of Lois) and was then roused to action.

Veteran director Curtiz was Wallis's choice to helm the project. The Hungarian had had difficulty in getting his own family out of the Nazi onslaught and wanted the picture badly. He was a bearish workaholic on the set but just as notoriously on time and under-budget. To bring out propagandistic properties in the material, he had some tinkering done by the Epstein brothers (Julius and Philip) before they were whisked to Washington to write real propaganda for Frank Capra's *Why We Fight* series for the War Department.

Lazlow was made a Czech. American Lois became Ilsa from Nazi-occupied Norway. In fact, sympathetic characters all through the script were given homelands at war with Germany or under German occupation. Only Rick in his French Moroccan

Café Americain could claim neutrality, hosting a strange world of conquerors and their conquered. And though the screenplay was conveniently set before Pearl Harbor and gave Rick a past that forbade him to go back home to enlist, wartime audiences were well aware of the underlying wake-up call implicit in lines like these:

RICK: Sam, if it's December in Casablanca, what time is it in New York?
SAM: My watch stopped.
RICK: I bet they're asleep in New York. I bet they're asleep all over America.

and wanted vengeance on Ilsa. Swedish Ingrid Bergman, who was borrowed from David O. Selznick to play this woman in the middle, had some concerns of her own: "All the time I wanted to know who I was supposed to be in love with. I didn't dare look at Humphrey Bogart with love because then I had to look at Paul Henreid with something that was not love." Curtiz told her to "just play it...in between." It's just as well that she did, for Bogart's spouse at that time, Mayo Methot, frequently made calls to the studio threatening to kill her husband if he didn't stop the affair she imagined he was having with Bergman.

Henreid, on the other hand, who that same year had made a romantic art out of lighting Bette Davis' cigarettes in *Now, Voyager* (1942), was jealous about a different kind of attention. Having insisted on equal billing with Bogart and Bergman, he was dis-

tinctly peeved when, during his climactic Marseillaise scene, Curtiz directed the Café Americain band musicians to look admiringly at Rick after Lazlow had done the conducting.

Egos aside, all went more or less smoothly after the April 11 start date until...the ending. Nothing seemed right. As the cast edged toward the unformed final scenes, hired-gun writer Howard Koch literally brought fresh pages to the soundstage for every shot. Sundays were spent at Curtiz's with Wallis, pages spread across the floor in search of a proper wrap-up.

Ronald Reagan was briefly considered for the heroic antihero, but Humphrey Bogart was the natural choice. With the character of Rick, Warner Brothers could romanticize Bogart's "man's man" image. Bogart himself lobbied for a more sympathetic character than the earlier versions of the screenplay, which had cast Rick as a philandering ex-lawyer who had left his wife, dumped his kids,

**LEFT: If Louis Renault (Claude Rains) looks a little uncomfortable giving orders to that gendarme it is because of what Rick Blain (Humphrey Bogart) has in his trenchcoat pocket, as right triumphs over love in Casablanca (1942).**
**ABOVE: Tobacco companies must have rejoiced at Paul Henreid's romantic way of lighting Bette Davis's cigarette in Now, Voyager (1942).**

**Sweet Misery, or Get Out Your Handkerchiefs   33**

**34 Sweet Misery, or Get Out Your Handkerchiefs**

They toyed with Rick leaving with Ilsa. They tried Ilsa staying with Rick. In one draft Rick was killed helping Lazlow escape. In another he went to jail for his heroism. Finally, the Epsteins blew back into town to save the day and everyone's sanity. They suggested that a newly patriotic, formerly Machiavellian police chief, Louis Renault (the ever-subtle Claude Rains), cover for Rick, allowing Lazlow to get away (with or without Ilsa). Henreid threatened to quit if Lazlow didn't get the girl, so Curtiz was ready to film two final scenes. After lensing the first version (you know, that noble, simply eloquent, and heartbreaking "hill of beans" moment at the airport, after which Rick and Louis walk off into the fog, the French Resistance, and "the beginning of a beautiful friendship"), Curtiz decided to let the second stay on the page. Bergman herself never knew the wrap-up until seeing it on the big screen, for after her exit she had immediately cut her hair and rushed to replace the lead in Paramount's *For Whom the Bell Tolls* (1943).

Though one test-audience member suggested a title change because it sounded too much like a beer, *Casablanca* was fortuitously released in 1942 just after the Allies had made their North African landing in Casablanca, of all places, and just before Churchill, Roosevelt, and Stalin held their conference in—you guessed it—Casablanca. The film's New York debut at the Hollywood Theater played to thirty-one thousand paid admissions in the first week alone.

Critics uniformly hailed *Casablanca* as a masterpiece as it took three major Oscars that year and was nominated for five others. Curtiz, as well known in Hollywood for butchery of his adopted tongue as for his brilliant direction, was in true form when accepting his Oscar. He emotionally said, "So many times I have a speech ready, but no dice. Always a bridesmaid never a mother. Now I win, I have no speech."

No speech was necessary. *Casablanca* not only became one of those few mythic romances that all other movies are measured against, but its shadowy and cynical style gave the go-ahead for the flood of the forties' "Film Noir" pictures. Rick and Ilsa may "always have Paris," but we'll always have *Casablanca*.

*Ingrid's new do for* **For Whom the Bell Tolls** *(1943) made reshoots for* **Casablanca** *(1942) impossible, thereby saving Dooley Wilson's rendition of the now immortal song, "As Time Goes By."*

# LOVE HURTS

There's something about the internal tempest of adolescence that's just prime for heartbreak. Bottle that volatile mixture into the moral straitjacket of small-town Americana that the playwright William Inge knew so well and you've got emotional dynamite.

*Splendor in the Grass* (1961) takes a bright, beautiful, and true-hearted Kansas high school senior named Wilma Dean Loomis (Deanie to her friends) and has her fall madly in love with a just-as-nice football player named Bud Stamper. So far so good. In the fat and happy 1928 postwar world of sock hops and rumble seats, Bud and Deanie would be king and queen of the prom, if it weren't for a few obstacles.

She is dirt poor and he's the richest boy in town. His father, Ace, is a bullheaded, steamrolling patriarch of an oil tycoon who believes that there are two kinds of women and sex is reserved for the other kind. Ace has already turned his own daughter, Ginny, into the other kind through repression and is determined to run his submissive son's life right into Yale or the ground. Deanie's mother, on the other hand, is a clinging harpy whose hatred of sex has already given Deanie a superego the size of Kansas and has reduced Deanie's father to a neutered jellyfish.

Bud and Deanie are soul mates, torn by their duty and their desires. But when push comes to shove, if she can't come through, there are other girls—less morally inclined girls—who would like a crack at the handsome, inarticulate, hormone-raging Bud. Bud's a little weak and Deanie, truth be told, is wound a little too tightly for her own good. A big fall is coming (along with the stock market crash) with no one but themselves to pick up the jagged pieces when it's over. And that won't be for each other.

It took five minutes for Inge to tell legendary director Elia Kazan a harrowing story along these lines from his Kansas youth during a stage rehearsal for *The Dark at the Top of the Stairs*. For two years they sent various revisions of the growing screenplay back and forth. Kazan knew about young people in love. He had already directed Marlon Brando and Eva Marie Saint as a principled palooka and a good girl with a spark in *On the Waterfront* (1954) as well as James Dean and Julie Harris as a bitter brother and the girl who loved him in John Steinbeck's *East of Eden* (1955). Luckily for us, he also knew just the extraordinary actors to pull off this Midwestern story (much of which, ironically, would be shot on Staten Island because it looked more like Kansas than Kansas did).

Warren Beatty made his movie debut as Bud, having just come from starring in an Inge play on Broadway. He admitted, "I'm a bit scared and worried but I'd try anything with Bill and Gadge (Kazan's nickname)." He loved the film script for its "feeling for young people" and its unpretentious language. The empathy shows in his portrayal of what Inge described as "an active, physical boy, cautiously raised and almost cursed with a conscience". There is no one Bud can turn to. His mother (Joanna Roos) is mush.

Though nothing can bring back the hour
Of splendour in the grass,
Glory in the flower,
We will grieve not, rather find
Strength in what remains behind.

—from "Ode on Intimations of Immortality"
by William Wordsworth

His doctor (John McGovern) won't acknowledge his request for help. His sister (Barbara Loden) lives only to torment her parents. And his father (Pat Hingle) is a back-slapping monster.

As muddled as Beatty's Bud is, Natalie Wood's Deanie is as clear and open as you can imagine a human being managing to be, and she pays the price for it. As Wood said, "So many nice girls in the movies are a bit on the dull side. Not this part—not Deanie." For all her sharpness, this good girl finds no corner—not with her shallow friends (Sandy Dennis, among others) at school, not with her jellyfish of a father (Del Loomis), not even in the privacy of her bathtub. The scene there where she fends off her tyrannical mother (Audrey Christie) and snaps in the process is truly shattering to watch.

As *Splendor in the Grass* unravels there is suicide, betrayal, a mental institution in Wichita, near rapes, near drownings, debauchery, and an undistilled loneliness such as has rarely been shown on the screen. These nice kids are going to suffer and we're going to suffer with them straight through to an ending that Kazan called "the truest of any love story I've ever found."

*Delicta maiorum immeritus lues. [Undeservedly you will atone for the sins of your father.]*

—Horace

Having braved her lifelong fear of water—swimming near a waterfall for the movie—as well as endangering her marriage to Robert Wagner over a prolonged affair with future legendary womanizer Warren Beatty (who was then courting Joan Collins), Wood didn't win an Oscar (while Inge did). She did do some of the riskiest soul-searching ever lensed. As Kazan later noted, "She worked like she was saving her life. She knew she had made a lot of bad pictures, that her career was in danger, and she wanted to right it before it was too late. She did." There's a bitter irony that Deanie would have appreciated: the name of the boat that didn't save Natalie Wood's life that fateful night in 1981 was called "The Splendour."

*OPPOSITE: If that looks like real passion in Natalie Wood's eyes, it probably is. Like so many costars before and since, she and Warren Beatty fell head-over-heels while filming the super-ego-over-id* Splendor in the Grass *(1961). BELOW: The same year saw the actress in an even more tragic film tryst with the urban counterpart (Richard Beymer) to her modern-day Juliet in the musical* West Side Story *(1961).*

# LOVE MEANS NEVER HAVING TO SAY YOU'RE SCHMALTZY

"What can you say about a twenty-five-year-old girl who died?" asks a bereaved Ryan O'Neal in one of the most wonderfully, shamelessly lachrymose films ever made. Well, you can say it made O'Neal a star. You can say it earned $2,400,000 in the first three days it played with almost no sex in it whatsoever. You can say Richard Nixon endorsed it. You can say that in 1972 there was a craze for couples in Warsaw, Poland, to get married to its tragic musical theme. You can say it was the film chosen for the

1971 Royal Command Performance attended by Queen Elizabeth. You can say that American literary giants William Styron and John Cheever threatened to resign when five hundred critics, librarians, and booksellers gave Erich Segal's novel the National Book Award. You can say it was not quite like any other movie ever made.

*Love Story* (1970) may be one of the most simplistic, manipulative, tear-jerking love stories ever wrought, but if you let it take you

for a ride you probably won't be able to cry again for the next few years. It is the tale of a refugee from a wealthy family, a Harvard law student and hockey-playing WASP, Oliver Barret III (O'Neal), who falls deeply in love with a harpsichord-playing, motherless, raven-haired, wide-eyed, smart-assed, working-class Radcliffe beauty named Jenny Cavaleri (Ali MacGraw). They joust wits as collegiate types do. They drop their guards as lovers do. They lash out against authority as sixties kids did. They struggle and scrimp as all young marrieds do. They succeed as all good people do. They find true happiness. She gets leukemia. 'Nuff said?

When Howard Minsky was an agent at William Morris in New York, a script came in from one of the agency's clients that nobody wanted, but that Minsky thought he'd use to take a crack at producing. It was a tragic love story about a nice Jewish girl from Brooklyn and a wealthy WASP.

Erich Segal had yet one more thing going for him. At Harvard he had done a production of *Much Ado About Nothing* with a Wellesley girl who had also designed sets while he did the play's music. She had gone on to dabble as an editorial assistant at *Harper's Bazaar*, work as a photographer's fashion stylist, and model for magazines like *Glamour*, *Seventeen*, and *Mademoiselle* before breaking into the movies in a big way as spoiled JAP Brenda Patimkin in the film of Phillip Roth's *Goodbye, Columbus* (1969). Her name was Ali MacGraw. She was a hot property and now married to Paramount's Vice President of Worldwide Distribution Robert Evans.

Through nine rewrites, Minsky got Segal to clean out the expletives as well as much of the nudity and reset it at Harvard. Literally every other major studio turned it down, but Ali loved it...and so did Paramount. They bought it for $75,000, $10,000 of which Segal and Minsky kicked back into publicity to match the studio's $10,000. It was a wise move. With the buildup it got, *The Ladies Home Journal* bought it as a serial. Harper Publishers published Segal's novelization ten months before the movie came out. By that time it was a sensation.

Why? This is one movie that's not afraid to feel. It plucks enough heartstrings to give Spielberg and Disney something to think about. As O'Neal said of his Oliver (dubbed "Preppie" by Jenny), "The guy I play has a great big heart. He's got a kind of vulnerability that's quite attractive in films today." That he has. His battle against his family and his fierce love for the arrogant-on-the-outside-but-vulnerable-on-the-inside Jenny is truly touching. Their frolics in the snow, walks in the rain, and horsing around in the frosty football stadium (all shot with the $25,000 left over from the scrimped $2,200,000 bud-

> *Thank God you wrote a nice book, not like Philip Roth.*
>
> —the response from Erich Segal's mother to his novelization of *Love Story*

don't want Paris. I don't need Paris. I just want you. And I need time. And that you can't give me"? The ending (don't be mad, you know she's dead from the beginning) is almost too much to bear, with MacGraw lying in a hospital bed. So what if she doesn't look that sick or, as *New York Times* critic Vincent Canby cattily said, "as if she were suffering from some vaguely unpleasant Elizabeth Arden treatment"? We are rooting so heavily for these youngsters that we're the goners.

The book may have had Oliver's tycoon father embracing his estranged son when Oliver rushes to meet his father after leaving

**ABOVE: She's an angel from heaven... and that's just where she's going. So, get ready to cry for Jenny Cavaleri (Ali MacGraw) or for the boy (Ryan O'Neal) she leaves behind in (sniff-sniff) Love Story (1970). OPPOSITE: Ali MacGraw's first starring role also cast her in a schmaltzy love affair, opposite Richard Benjamin in Goodbye Columbus (1969).**

get) are just what you wish your college days had been.

In other words, the kids have heart. How else could they get away with lines like, "Love means never having to say you're sorry," or "I care," or "I Jenny's side. But in the words of director Arthur Hiller, "If we had the father and son embrace most of the audience would have to be carried out." As it was, O'Neal and MacGraw were both so worked up by the final hospital scene that Hiller had to shoot several takes just to get their grief under control—and that was with the precaution of not shooting in a real hospital. Such is the power of this story.

*Love Story* broke house records for attendance in 159 of the 165 theaters in which it opened, earning $9,000,000 in just two weeks. It made stars of O'Neal and MacGraw and earned Minsky a percentage so great that he said, "I won't be able to spend it in my lifetime." It also provided O'Neal with a lesson in irony. All through the shooting Hiller remembers, "I kept telling Ryan that he must make the audience believe he would never have a relationship with another girl." Well, ahem...eight years later Oliver tried to forget the past with equally smart-assed Candice Bergen in *Oliver's Story* (1978). The rest of us (sniff! sniff!) can't forget.

# THE LADY SWOONS

*Jenny Cavaleri wasn't the only lover cut down in her prime. See if you can match up the terminal or otherwise afflicted tragediennes and their plots with the movies that have moved millions to tears.*

## DAMAS

1. She's got cancer and an overbearing mother who's in love with Jack Nicholson.
2. She didn't count on falling for him when his family hired her to help him with chemotherapy treatments.
3. She's got cancer and a new Brit boyfriend who writes kids' books.
4. Consumptive or not, this French courtesan has what it takes to rob Robert Taylor from the cradle.
5. She's a famous actress who can't have kids, but adopting might be a problem with a terminal heart condition.
6. Her death in childbirth might make up for causing the demise of her sister's child.
7. She's a deaf mute who was raped by the town bully and now nice doctor Lew Ayers is getting the blame.
8. She is one headstrong heiress until she finds out there's something very unfriendly growing in her head and goes head over heels for her doctor.
9. This waitress wants to share much more than tips with a busboy with a heart condition.
10. She's a concert pianist with suicidal tendencies and one boyfriend who likes to smash her hands with a cane.
11. This debutante loses her hearing from meningitis on the night of her engagement party.
12. She's an Olympic-class skier whose fall leaves her paralyzed from the shoulders down.
13. She was crippled from a ski accident and Joseph Cotten, the man responsible, is now her caretaker.
14. She's a Swiss sanitarium patient who has lured grand prix driver Al Pacino off course.
15. She's plain ugly, but life with a disfigured pilot could still be paradise.
16. Imagine wedding a war amnesia victim only to have him get knocked out, remember his old life, and forget all about you.
17. This terminally ill pianist is the perfect girlfriend for an R.A.F. pilot who's losing his eyesight.

## DRAMAS

A: Lizabeth Scott in **Paid in Full** *(1950)*
B: Debra Winger in **Shadowlands** *(1993)*
C: Greer Garson in **Random Harvest** *(1942)*
D: Marilyn Hassett in **The Other Side of the Mountain** *(1975)*
E: Ann Todd in **The Seventh Veil** *(1945)*
F: Greta Garbo in **Camille** *(1937)*
G: Alida Valli in **Walk Softly, Stranger** *(1950)*
H: Bette Davis in **Dark Victory** *(1939)*
I: Loretta Young in **And Now Tomorrow** *(1944)*
J: Maureen O'Hara in **Sentimental Journey** *(1946)*
K: Marisa Tomei in **Untamed Heart** *(1993)*
L: Marthe Keller in **Bobby Deerfield** *(1977)*
M: Jane Wyman in **Johnny Belinda** *(1948)*
N: Dorothy McGuire in **The Enchanted Cottage** *(1945)*
O: Julia Roberts in **Dying Young** *(1991)*
P: Debra Winger in **Terms of Endearment** *(1983)*
Q: Margaret Lockwood in **Love Story** *(1944)*

**Answers**

1=P, 2=O, 3=B, 4=F, 5=I, 6=A, 7=M, 8=H, 9=K, 10=E, 11=I, 12=D, 13=G, 14=L, 15=N, 16=C, 17=Q

# We'll Always Have Iowa

Robert Waller's 172-page, unabashedly romantic tearjerker, *The Bridges of Madison County*, may have been snubbed by the *Los Angeles Times* as "like a Coke that's been opened a while: sweet but flat," but that didn't stop it from selling like sweet, flat hotcakes—$9,500,000 worth of copies worldwide and 148 weeks on the *New York Times* best-seller list, earning its author a reported $26,000,000. It didn't stop at least one thousand crazed callers from being so swept up that they contacted the National Geographic Society to find the whereabouts of the book's fictional hero, Robert Kincaid. Nor did it stop Hollywood's biggest player, Steven Spielberg, from snapping up the rights for an additional $275,000 before the book was even published.

Lili Zanuck called Clint Eastwood up one day and asked him if he had read the best-seller about the middle-aged, wandering, manfully sensitive, erotically expert *National Geographic* photographer who stops in for water at an Iowa farmhouse while on assignment to shoot covered bridges and unexpectedly meets the love of his life—a neglected Italian farm wife whose family has gone away for a week to a state fair. Eastwood admitted that he had only heard about it. Zanuck replied, "Read it because you're in it."

Spielberg's plans to direct the lanky star changed with his need for a break after *Schindler's List* (1993). Writer Richard LaGravenese had already adapted Waller's schmaltzathon to bring it back to reality and fill the previously sketchy character of Francesca with delightful anger and humor. Sydney Pollack took the reins for a while, wanting to work with Robert Redford and Mary McDonnell, but Clint was part of the package now and with *Driving Miss Daisy* (1989) director Bruce Beresford next in line, new conflicts arose.

Beresford didn't cotton to the edgier tone of the treatment and wanted the substantially younger Isabella Rossellini for Francesca. Spielberg's Amblin, which was still producing, wanted even younger actresses. Eastwood finally balked. At a grizzled sixty-five (thirteen years older than Kincaid), he needed a mature partner to play to. When Beresford backed out over their differences, Eastwood took over direction and called forty-six-year-old Meryl Streep, who had just made *The River Wild* (1994) to show her three daughters that buffed action heroes could be women.

Streep's baby-sitter picked up the phone at her employer's home in Connecticut to hear a voice rasp, "This is Clint Eastwood." She laughed, assuming it was Streep's practical-joker father, and scolded, "Harry, I know who this is!" As Streep remembers, "It's a miracle I got the part."

The ten-time Oscar nominee had in her own words been "blind to the book's power." Eastwood was up front on the phone, saying, "I know you're not interested in this and I've heard that you don't like it. But maybe you might be interested in reading this treatment that this writer has done. I really want you to read it." Streep obliged and ended up weeping before she finished it the next morning. LaGravenese's treatment had made the invisible character of the wife "visible" to her. She dried her eyes long enough to call Clint with a "yes" that afternoon.

Eastwood was committed to making his film "as simple and straightforward as the book. I wanted to do it in sequence, so that the actors' relationships could develop as naturally as the

> I think that Clint told the story in a way that I wouldn't have told the story and I think he told the story better than I could have told the story.... I think he did a wonderful job of not pushing all the buttons.
>
> —Steven Spielberg on *The Bridges of Madison County* (1995)

> I only made one call.
>
> —Clint Eastwood on casting the role of Francesca in *The Bridges of Madison County*

characters." His own experience in action pictures had made him dissatisfied with films that try to "quick get the dialogue out so we can get to some movement, when there is a lot of real time between people when they're just standing there talking." There would be no special effects, no matte shots, no superimpositions, and only nine weeks of shooting.

Streep was thrilled when she learned she would get to shoot in sequence. Her own five-week shooting schedule ("I was home a month before I got a paycheck") was also fine with the actress who, though often labeled as a technical virtuoso on projects lasting for months, has almost always enjoyed the first reading of a scene more than anything subsequent. As Streep has more bluntly said, "I come ready and I don't want to screw around and waste time the first ten takes on adjusting the lights and everybody else getting comfortable."

It was, if not a marriage, a love affair made in heaven. "Clint has a group of people that he has worked with for a number of years and everyone knows exactly what he wants," admitted Streep. "They are really, really ready, more so than any other group that I've seen in my life. Part of this is the tension of knowing that he may just shoot the rehearsal and move. He isn't going to explore this forty times. It's a very live, respectful, attentive set, and he is the effortless captain of the ship."

Things did indeed flow on the set where Eastwood commented that Streep—"like Gene Hackman and Morgan Freeman"—was "just one of those people who are ready to roll." An abandoned, dilapidated, two-story white Victorian farmhouse was rented for a small fee. Cats were used to kill all the field mice inside (until Clint's allergies kicked up). The crew waded through decades of raccoon turds to clean the place up and production designer Jeanine Oppewall poured $500,000 into renovations.

In this bucolic paradise, Streep, whose *River Wild* white-water muscles had softened a bit ("I don't think anybody has shot a love story weighing as much as I did"), roamed the set not in tight jeans and a T-shirt as the book's heroine did, but barefoot in the kind of simple cotton housedresses that Eastwood remembered his own mother wearing decades before. She liked them so much, in fact, that she kept them after the shoot.

The chemistry that develops between Eastwood's Kincaid and Streep's Francesca, despite a few holdover cornball lines of dialogue to satisfy book fans, is deeply moving and deeply personal. Streep is as flawlessly real and compelling (adding yet another effortless foreign accent to her collection) as the woman who discovers the gypsy in her soul as Eastwood is as the gypsy who realizes that there is finally someone worth settling down for. Though initially uneasy about being partnered with an actor who might directorially detach himself during crucial moments, Streep "felt completely locked in as an actor" with Eastwood's Kincaid. Although as a director "he didn't really speak to me for the first half of the film, and I was getting alarmed," she further admitted, "Finally, one day he said, 'You know I don't say much unless I don't like it.'"

As Eastwood describes it, "These people are misfits. As their friendship develops they realize how much they appreciate each other and how much was missing from their lives. The emotion comes later. It heightens everything when they are together and it becomes almost unbearable when they try to separate." The separation scene may be the reason that the Sony theater in Manhattan's Lincoln Square had a box of tissues on hand on top of the popcorn dispenser. "Except for forty-five minutes at lunch," boasted makeup man J. Roy Hellan, "the tears were flowing for two days. There's no glycerin with Meryl. When she cries she cries." She wasn't alone. As director of photography Jack N. Green remembers, "I'd try to brush them [tears] away when no one was looking, then I'd turn around and see Clint doing the same. Everyone was trying to look like they weren't crying when they were."

Like the grips and the burly teamsters on the set, you may well need a few minutes to compose yourself before heading back to life after Iowa, for with all due respect to Bening and Beatty, here truly is a love affair to remember. As to the inevitable rumors that life may have imitated art on the set, the stars are anything but teary. When asked to confirm the gossip, you can well imagine Eastwood narrowing his eyes as he rasps, "Meryl? She lives in Connecticut, she's got a family." And Streep makes it even plainer: "It's not even worth responding to," she says. "It's like, 'I can't act this'?" They certainly can.

**OPPOSITE: Things look sunny now (or do they?), but just you wait. Lovers have rarely been as star-crossed as Sophie the concentration camp survivor (Meryl Streep) and Nathan the pseudo-scientist (Kevin Kline) in Sophie's Choice (1982). ABOVE: A toast from the heart, though not to tomorrow, as photographer Clint Eastwood and Italian housewife Meryl Streep grab happiness while they can in The Bridges of Madison County (1995).**

# To Prove My Love For You

Sure you watch the weepy movies, but do you know what real commitment is all about? Talk is cheap. The next time someone asks you to prove your love, what are you going to do—share the remote? See if you can match up the movie with the heroic acts of self-sacrifice. You might even get some ideas for proving your worth somewhere down the road of romance.

## IF YOU REALLY LOVED ME YOU'D

1. take the long swim to China to make sure my screen career doesn't drown in your drink

2. eat a strawberry you're deathly allergic to just to show how much you trust me

3. perjure yourself into a murder rap to save me from the hot seat

4. poison yourself while infiltrating a Nazi spy ring to win my respect

5. put down your cherished Quaker pacifism and pick up a rifle to save my skin

6. free all the wild mustangs you've caught for the glue factory

7. write my boyfriend's love poems though you love me more and grow old with the secret

8. hoof it to Russia to get me out of a revolting situation

9. play a little Russian roulette to bring me back to my senses and hopefully back to the United States

10. relinquish custody of our kid after you've dumped us both

11. take the murder rap for me even though the victim was your ex-girlfriend and I'm something else altogether

12. take the long swim to China so as not to get in the way of my new romance

13. fink on the Mob because you set my brother up for a fall

14. rip off your protective helmet to let me touch your face even though I've got the plague

15. relive my gruesome death (from my perspective) just to bring my killer to justice

16. come back from the dead to convince me you're not worth that much grief

17. wipe out my pimp (and everyone else in the vicinity) to save my twelve-year-old virtue

18. keep the secret of my baby after a one-night stand and let me obliviously woo you all over again years later

19. risk deevolving to pull me out of the primal mists

20. chase me down to Hades just to bring me back

21. impregnate my best friend

22. sleep with my sleazy boss to steal something I need to stay alive

23. make me pregnant so that your impotent uncle will stop beating me and then agree to pretend that it's his kid

24. carry me up to the top of the RKO tower (King Kong style) when the aliens come to zap me

25. bust me and my buddy out of prison even though you are the warden's wife

26. fight to be part of my paraplegic life even though I pretend I don't want to have anything to do with you

27. dress in drag as my wife because my son is marrying the daughter of a stuffy bureaucrat

**A:** *Grace Kelly did for Gary Cooper in* High Noon *(1952)*

**B:** *Jeff Bridges did for Isabella Rossellini in* Fearless *(1993)*

**C:** *Robert De Niro did for Christopher Walken in* The Deer Hunter *(1978)*

**D:** *Teresa Wright did for Marlon Brando in* The Men *(1950)*

**E:** *Clark Gable did for Marilyn Monroe in* The Misfits *(1961)*

**F:** *James Mason did for Judy Garland in* A Star Is Born *(1954)*

**G:** *Bruce Dern did for Jane Fonda in* Coming Home *(1978)*

**H:** *Diane Keaton did for Warren Beatty in* Reds *(1981)*

**I:** *Ingrid Bergman did for Cary Grant in* Notorious *(1946)*

**J:** *Jeanne Tripplehorn did for Tom Cruise in* The Firm *(1993)*

**K:** *Stephen Rea did for Jaye Davidson in* The Crying Game *(1992)*

**L:** *Li Bao-Tian did for Gong Li in* Ju Dou *(1989)*

**M:** *Robert De Niro did for Jodie Foster in* Taxi Driver *(1976)*

**N:** *Dustin Hoffman did for Rene Russo in* Outbreak *(1995)*

**O:** *Michel Serrault did for Ugo Tognazzi in* La Cage aux Folles *(1978)*

**P:** *Blair Brown did for William Hurt in* Altered States *(1980)*

**Q:** *Marlon Brando did for Eva Marie Saint in* On the Waterfront *(1954)*

**R:** *Peter Hinwood did for Tim Curry in* The Rocky Horror Picture Show *(1975)*

**S:** *Marlene Dietrich did for Tyrone Power in* Witness for the Prosecution *(1957)*

**T:** *Alan Rickman did for Juliet Stevenson in* Truly Madly Deeply *(1991)*

**U:** *Ray Liotta did for Caroline Elliott in* Unforgettable *(1996)*

**V:** *Gerard Depardieu did for Anne Brochet in* Cyrano de Bergerac *(1990)*

**W:** *Kevin Kline did for Glenn Close in* The Big Chill *(1983)*

**X:** *Breno Mello did for Marpessa Dawn in* Black Orpheus *(1959)*

**Y:** *Meryl Streep did for Dustin Hoffman in* Kramer vs. Kramer *(1979)*

**Z:** *Diane Keaton did for Mel Gibson in* Mrs. Soffel *(1984)*

**AA:** *Joan Fontaine did for Louis Jourdan in* Letter from an Unknown Woman *(1948)*

**Answers**

1=F, 2=B, 3=S, 4=I, 5=A, 6=E, 7=V, 8=H, 9=C, 10=Y, 11=K, 12=G, 13=Q, 14=N, 15=U, 16=T, 17=M, 18=AA, 19=P, 20=X, 21=W, 22=J, 23=L, 24=R, 25=Z, 26=D, 27=O

# LAST CHANCE
# FOR LOVE

*U*na Giornata Particulare (A Special Day), winner of the jury prize at the 1977 Cannes film festival, starred two actors who weren't exactly strangers to each other. As well as being long time friends, Sophia Loren and Marcello Mastroianni had already starred in seven films together by the late seventies. In *Too Bad She's Bad* (1954) she had been a cab stealer to his taxi driver. In *The Miller's Wife* (1955) a lustful, corrupt Neopolitan governor, had tried to win his wife's favors. In *Lucky to Be a Woman* (1955) it was his turn to try to win her from Charles Boyer after he had taken a photograph of her adjusting her stockings that made her a national sex symbol.

In the three episodes of *Yesterday, Today and Tomorrow* (1963) he was alternately: the underemployed husband who had to get his wife pregnant seven times in order to protect her from the authorities for selling contraband cigarettes; a struggling writer wooing the mink-toting Milanese wife of a wealthy industrialist; and a frustrated Bologna playboy to her call girl who had taken a one-week vow of chastity under the influence of a seminary student. *Marriage Italian*

*Style* (1964) brought her to her deathbed as his longtime mistress, whom he now had to marry to save her soul. She remarried someone else after he had been sent to the Russian front in *Sunflower* (1969). Perhaps most outrageously, she was an ex-rock singer making life difficult for his simple padre in *The Priest's Wife* (1970).

The two superstars had been many things to each other by middle age. They had also become icons of desirability to millions of filmgoers. There weren't many women who didn't rank Mastroianni's noble forehead, quizzical eyes, or curling lip as musts for any Latin lover fantasy. Not many other married men would be able to claim lovers like Catherine Deneuve, Brigitte Bardot, Faye Dunaway, and Nastassja Kinski. There weren't many men who didn't see the voluptuous Sophia, whether costumed in revealing peasant rags or royal finery, as the passionate mistress of their imaginations. Nor had many other forty-three-year-old sex symbols won Academy Awards for their acting, as Sophia had (at the age of twenty-six) in Vittorio De Sica's unforgettable war story, *Two Women* (1960).

So, when De Sica's directoral heir apparent, Ettore Scola, planned a small-scale film about a tragic tryst between a bedraggled housewife and an effete homosexual one May afternoon in 1939 when Adolph Hitler came to Rome, his casting may have surpised some. What surprised more is that his two Italian celebrities did some of the least glamorous and most intimate acting ever to grace a screen.

*Perhaps my physique is that of a gallant hero, but I've always felt more at ease when I have been able to interpret the characteristics of an individual rather than simply having to represent his physical attractiveness.*

**—Marcello Mastroianni**

*A Special Day* begins with an oppresive presence which we will never quite get away from, the documented sights and sounds of Hitler's visit to fascist Italy. In an opening tracking shot that lasts a full five-and-a-half minutes, we penetrate a dingy apartment building to follow Loren's perpetually haggard housewife (no makeup for this role) and matrimonially subjugated mother of six kids ("with seven you get a medal," she later says), Antonetta, as she rousts her brood and brooding, brutish husband (the kind of guy who dries his hands on her dress) for the special day ahead. Only after her unfeeling family trundles off to see the two dictators without her is she at leisure to drink their coffee dregs and clean up after the seven of them. Her loneliness, despair, and resignation are palpable.

When her pet mynah bird, Rosmunda, flies out the window to the opposite window ledge, Antonetta runs across the empty complex to catch her. At the apartment directly across the plaza from hers, she barges in on Gabriel (Mastroianni), a recently fired radio DJ who is about to commit suicide. Momentarily rescued from his desperation, he helps her recover the bird with a broom (it actually took twenty-seven takes, and the bird had to have its beak and claws taped to

keep it from scratching Sophia's breast; and it whistled the Communist national anthem at the most inappropriate times). Grateful to be away from the precipice, Gabriel offers his visitor the copy of *The Three Musketeers* he sees her spying (she never has any time to read). Frumpy Antonetta balks at his attempt to teach her the rhumba steps he's been practicing. Though they could both use the company, she flees back to her domestic duties. But he follows with the book. And so begins the tentative journey of two strangers towards each other during one afternoon. So begins some seriously lachrymose movie magic.

There are so many miraculous moments in this two-person film that it almost defies explanation. Somehow, set against the background blare and radio reminder of the fascist world they live in, Loren and Mastroianni unfold in each other's presence like flowers exposed to light after years of darkness.

**LEFT: Sophia Loren feels the heat but Marcello Mastroianni has his reasons for being lukewarm in the human, touching, shattering film, A Special Day (1977).**
**ABOVE: The neglected housewife and the radio radical, a mismatch made in heaven under the shadow of Il Duce for A Special Day (1977).**

He confides in her about the humiliation of being fired and the solitude tax he pays for being single ("as if solitude was valuable"). She awkwardly shows him her Il Duce scrapbook and is flummoxed to learn that he is a feminist and anti-fascist. He both exasperates and delights her by riding her son's scooter around her apartment. Accompanying her to the roof to fold laundry, he makes her laugh for perhaps the first time in a decade and mischievously hugs her through a sheet he's dropped on her. But Antonetta misconstrues this as a come-on, and when she responds with pent-up passion, he bursts her lonely bubble. This dapper, handsome, humorous, human man is gay.

The end? No, only the begining. The chain reaction of anger, pain, and honesty this moment ignites in both of them takes things to a whole new level. From here on in, all the cards get placed on the table and love becomes as transformational as it is tragic. As *Time* magazine critic Frank Rich admitted, "When Loren addresses the camera with this much intensity, no audience in its right mind would turn away." Just try. By the final shot, which is almost as long as the opening, you had better make sure you have an ample supply of *fazzoletti* on hand (that's Italian for hankies). You have witnessed a very special day, indeed.

*Catholic Marguerite de Valois (Isabel Adjani) and protestant Henri de Navarre (Daniel Auteuil) are a marriage made in court, not heaven, and vows or no vows, blood will flow in* Queen Margot *(1994).*

# DOWN WITH LOVE

*In my whole life I never had a woman so in love with me as Ingrid Bergman was. The day the picture [Saratoga Trunk] ended, I couldn't get her on the phone.*
—Gary Cooper

*I have never loved anyone like Gary Cooper, and I never will again. He was the most gorgeous, attractive man I've ever known. When Gary and I were finished, I was broken hearted.*
—Patricia Neal

*I proposed to Piper Laurie while we were doing retakes on* The Golden Blade. *I said, "Piper, after this picture is over let's go to Mexico. Of course, we'll have to be married." I guess that wasn't the way to frame a marriage proposal properly. She said, "Thank you. And now let's get back to work."*
—Rock Hudson

*I was a bridesmaid at Liz Taylor's wedding, and she was a bridesmaid at mine. It's a good thing we stopped there or it would have turned into a full-time job.*
—Jane Powell

*It really shook me up when Trigger passed on. It was like losing one of the family.*
—Roy Rogers

*And Mia Farrow? Hah! I always knew Frank [Sinatra] would end up in bed with a boy.*
—Ava Gardner

*My dear, he would have your hand while looking into your eyes and rubbing his leg on somebody else's leg at the same time, while having the gate man phone him before his wife arrived.*
—Joan Blondell on Leslie Howard

*By the time I made* The Charge of the Light Brigade *I was sure I was in love with her. Olivia [de Havilland] was only 21 then. I was married, of course, unhappily. Olivia was lovely — and distant. She must have actively disliked me for the teasing I did, for I sprang some very obstreperous gags. There was the time she found a dead snake in her panties as she was about to put them on. She knew very well who was responsible and it couldn't have endeared me to her. It slowly penetrated my obtuse head that such juvenile pranks weren't the way to a girl's heart. But it was too late. I couldn't soften her.*
—Errol Flynn

*Marry an outdoor woman. Then if you have to throw her out in the yard for the night, she can still survive.*
—W. C. Fields

*Men fall in love with Gilda and wake up with me.*
—Rita Hayworth

*In an agent's office, I overheard an actor say that Margaret O' Sullivan was having an affair with the producer, Jed Harris...I'd lean against the fence and I'd stare up at our apartment with the lighted windows on the second floor. I knew Harris was inside with her and I'd wait for him to leave. But instead the lights would go out. More nights than I'd care to remember I'd stand there and cry...I couldn't believe my wife and that son-of-a-bitch were in bed together. But I knew they were. And that just destroyed me.*
—Henry Fonda

# Chapter Three

# LOVE IS A MANY SPLINTERED THING, OR GET OUT YOUR THERAPISTS

*You always hurt
the one you love*

**—Doris Fisher and Allan Roberts**

Not even a hooker-with-a-heart-of-gold can save this kamikaze boozer from himself. Elizabeth Shue and Nicolas Cage go out on a limb and take us right along with them in the risky, *riveting* Leaving Las Vegas (1995).

Turn on your television just about any late afternoon or early evening and do a little channel-surfing. CLICK: "Moms who seduce their daughters' prom dates—next on Oprah!" CLICK: "Meet the fan who's collected 217 discarded pieces of Whitney Houston's intimate apparel—tonight at eleven!" CLICK: "First he stole his best friend's girl. Then he changed his sex and stole his best friend's heart—on Jenny Jones!" CLICK: "Sally Jessy will be right back with more hot dating tips from her closed-circuit guests, Amy Fisher, Heidi Fleiss, and Mike Tyson, after this message." OK, OK, so the examples are bogus. But how far off the mark are they?

Today, who needs fiction? In an age when hundreds of thousands tune in day after day to view the legal aftermath of the bloody aftermath of a relationship gone terribly wrong, we're not all looking at the divine side of human nature. When movies of the week and supermarket tabloids are filled with suicide pacts, celebrity stalkings, lethal lovers' quarrels, and every other twist on Cupid's arrow, it's hard to deny that love gone bad has a powerful allure. Yet perhaps to see ourselves at our most imperfect is to see ourselves at our most human—comical, touching, or tragic.

For instance, when a chalk-dusted, eggheaded academic type discovers his or her buried libido in response to an earthy, emotive, sensual type, the results usually run one of two ways. One way can be comical if you're Henry Fonda falling for con woman Barbara Stanwyck in *The Lady Eve* (1941), Gary Cooper falling for chanteuse Stanwyck in *Ball of Fire* (1941), or Woody Allen falling for call girl Mira Sorvino in *Mighty Aphrodite* (1995). It can also be touching if you're Bette Davis falling for suave Paul Henreid in *Now, Voyager* (1942), Maggie Smith falling for sculptor Gordon Jackson in *The Prime of Miss Jean Brodie* (1969), or Smith falling for gangster Bob Hoskins in *The Lonely Passion of Judith Hearne* (1987).

Then there are those grisly exceptions, where things get way out of control. Occasionally, the academic is so tightly wound and the animal force so fierce that every layer of reason is unraveled. The moth flies directly into the flame and...z-z-z-z-t-t-t!

# THE DEVIL IN A BLUE DRESS

In 1929, the supremely arrogant yet supremely talented German director Josef von Sternberg (complete with riding crop and monocle) was on the prowl. He had been hired by Hollywood's Paramount and Germany's UFA studios to make a film (in German and in English) with a German star who would rival the international allure of the recent MGM discovery, Greta Garbo.

> *Ich kenne mich auch nicht und Gott soll mich auch davor behueten. [I do not know myself, and God forbid that I should.]*
>
> —Goethe

The story, Professor Unrath: "Downfall of a Tyrant," detailed the piteous decline of a middle-aged boys' school martinet who storms off to a local nightclub (the Blue Angel) to reprimand the lusty chanteuse of whom his students have been passing lewd postcards in class. The professor righteously confronts the vixen in her dressing room (where she has no qualms about undressing in front of him), but succumbs to her charms. Intrigued, fascinated, obsessed, he becomes an avid patron to her scandalously sexy act. Enmeshed even further, he marries her, loses his job in the ensuing scandal, goes on tour with her cheesy troupe, runs a gambling house, and is ultimately imprisoned for it.

For the love-enslaved professor, Sternberg secured the services of Emil Jannings, the star of F.W. Murnau's history-making tragedy, *The Last Laugh* (1924). The siren, Lola-Lola, would have to be a fresh face with a sensuality as vulgar as it was captivating.

The director saw hundreds of actresses in what was one of the most publicized talent hunts the movie industry had ever seen. One night he was having dinner at the Hotel Bristol, eating roast beef with future Third Reich documentarian Leni Riefenstahl, when he bemoaned the fruitlessness of his search and mentioned a name in passing—Marlene Dietrich. He hadn't seriously considered this brunette veteran of twenty-six stage productions and seventeen films, but friends had been telling him to see her in her latest play, *Zwie Krawatten* (Two Bow Ties).

Riefenstahl, an ex-hoofer herself, responded, "Marlene Dietrich, you say? I've seen her only once and was struck by her. She was sitting in a café with some young actresses, and my attention was drawn by her deep, coarse voice. Maybe she was a little tipsy. I heard her say in a loud voice, 'Why must we always have beautiful bosoms? Why can't they hang a little?' with which she lifted up her left breast and amused herself with it, startling the young girls sitting around her. She might be a good type for you."

Sternberg went to the Berliner Theater, where Dietrich not only performed but came out during intermission as the jazz baby, "Dollar Princess," to announce the lottery winners in English.

"Toulouse-Lautrec would have turned a couple of handsprings," he wryly rejoiced, and he called her for an interview. When the veteran performer arrived, she assumed it was to read for a bit part, having been snubbed for the lead, and she brought some attitude with her. Sternberg matched it, asking Dietrich why he had heard such dismal reports on her career. She flippantly responded that she photographed badly and was unlucky with the press. She agreed to Sternberg's screen test if he agreed to see three of her films, and mentioned that she had seen his work and that he didn't know how to direct women.

Sternberg saw the films and noted, "She was an awkward, unattractive woman, left to her own devices, and presented an embarrassing exhibition of drivel. Ice cold water was poured on me." But he also saw a face that, if exposed to his Svengaliesque guidance, "promised everything." Dietrich insolently showed up for the screen test without a costume, musical material, or a pianist as accompaniment. Sternberg hastily pinned her into the oversize

spangled costume she selected from his stock ("roomy enough to contain a hippopotamus"), curled her hair, and surrounded her with fake smoke.

Dietrich draped her shapely gams over the top of the piano and smokily sang "Wer Wird Denn Winen?" ("Why Cry? There's Another One on the Corner") as the cameras rolled. When asked for an English number, she accompanied herself to "You're the Cream in My Coffee." After the subsequent reading, Sternberg ecstatically noted, "She came to life and responded to my instruc-

**OPPOSITE: In tamer times out-of-whack relationships were the turf of temptress Barbara Stanwyck taking simple beer scion Henry Fonda for a hilarious ride in Preston Sturges' sterling comedy The Lady Eve (1941). ABOVE: Hussies come in all colors. Here, chanteuse Dorothy Dandridge wraps soldier boy Harry Belafonte around her little finger, and there will be hell to pay in the musical Carmen Jones (1954).**

*Love is a Many Splintered Thing, or Get Out Your Therapists* **53**

tions with an ease that I never before had encountered....The theater was in her blood and she was familiar with every parasite in it. Her energy to survive and rise above her environment must have been fantastic. Never before had I met so beautiful a woman who had been so thoroughly discounted and undervalued." Had the martinet found his muse? Or was it a smart actress who knew a director who appreciated languid arrogance equal to his own? Either way, Dietrich is said to have "ordered so much champagne you could bathe in it" when she learned she had got the role.

An aroused Sternberg made some major changes in his script. Worse than running a gambling house, Professor Unrath would com-pletely degenerate under the spell of his Teutonic temptress, enduring every humiliation from selling those same dirty postcards of his wife to playing an egg-laying clown to suffering her voracious infidelity to the nightmare of coming back to play the very town where his name was now a mockery. Even the name of the film was changed to that of the smoky club, *The Blue Angel* (1930). Sternberg changed Lola into a carnal automaton who couldn't help seducing and destroying men, though Jannings warned the younger actress that if she played it that way she would be through with films.

Dietrich embraced Sternberg's obsessive image, even on the set. As celebrated visitors like Buster Keaton, Sergei Eisenstein, and Max Reinhardt dropped by to visit the infamous set, Sternberg (who was carrying on his own affair with the married Dietrich) claimed he had to stop his star repeatedly for exposing more than just her cross-gartered legs to her audience during her sensual musical numbers. He also took infinite care to make that "promising" face shine. A newly blonde Dietrich was frequently lit from above, emphasizing her brow and diminishing the size of her nose. In some close-ups he arranged three "dinkies" (tiny spotlights) to meet just above her brow line to make it even more pronounced. A custom-made Rosher "bull's-eye" lens (which had been used originally for Mary Pickford) replicated the human eye, seeing what was in focus in sharp detail while softening every feature in the periphery.

This Lola she-devil did indeed look like a glowing angel. In scene after scene rarely needing more than one take, through the weblike layers of set that would become a Sternberg trademark, she coolly toyed with her blustering professor. Jannings, as manfully as he was acting, woke up to the fact that it was no longer his film. (This fact might have been precipitated when Heinrich Mann told Jannings, "The success of this film will be found in the naked thighs of Miss Dietrich.") He came to blows with the composer over a silence inserted after the famous "Falling in Love Again" number that was designed to permit applause. He became so enraged watching rushes one day that he was overheard muttering, "I'll strangle her"—and he almost did. In the chilling climactic scene of his breakdown, Jannings throttled his costar so violently that makeup had to be applied for retakes to cover the bruises on her throat. Dietrich had to wear a velvet choker that night for her stage performance in *Zwie Krawatten*.

It would have taken strangling to dull Dietrich's fire in the finished product, but Jannings shone just as fiercely. His descent is as dizzying and total as her allure is effortless and amoral. On April 1, 1930, the opening night at Berlin's Gloria-Palast Theater, the curtain calls for the stars were loud enough to disrupt traffic on the streets outside.

Sternberg had his own fire raging over his new "creation." He once boasted, "Her behavior on my stage was a marvel to behold. Her attention was riveted on me. No property master could have been more alert. She behaved as if she were my servant, first to notice that I was looking about for a pencil, first to rush for a chair when I wanted to sit down. Not the slightest resistance was offered to my domination of her performance." The master and his servant sailed for the United States and six more films together in the next five years. And though Dietrich always credited her master completely with her success, it's the servant today that is still remembered.

**OPPOSITE: Falling in love again? School teacher Emil Jannings may get a young Marlene Dietrich to strip, but she'll strip him of every shred of dignity before The Blue Angel (1930) is over. RIGHT: Guess who, Pop? Or would you rather feel your way toward an answer? Nymphet Sue Lyon embraces stepfather James Mason in Stanley Kubrick's perfectly perverse Lolita (1962).**

# THE DEVIL IN A BLUE JUMPER

When the opening credits for a movie show a close-up of a man's hands lovingly, servilely tucking cotton balls between the toes of a shapely adolescent foot that the man is about to daintily dab polish on— all to the swelling strains of Nelson Riddle's romantic piano—you know you're in store for something about a beauty salon or something much sleazier. In 1962, Stanley Kubrick took the second choice and did the impossible. Even the movie posters (which showed a sweet young face in heart-shaped sunglasses sucking a lollipop) begged the question, "How could they ever make a movie of 'Lolita'?"

In 1938, Vladimir Nabokov had started a short story in Russian called "The Enchantress," the rapturous prison confessional of a divorced French academic whose formative experience with a twelve-year-old nymphet left him with a fascination for girl flesh. The story recounted how, as he came to America for a teaching stint at Ohio's Beardsley College, he decided to summer in Ramsdale, New Hampshire, and look for lodgings. He was just about to opt out of a room in the house of a somewhat bovine, man-hungry widow with cultural pretensions named Charlotte Haze when he spied her bikini-bedecked twelve-year-old daughter,

> *It was perfectly all right for me to imagine a twelve-year-old Lolita. She only existed in my head. But to make a twelve-year-old girl play such a part in public would be sinful and immoral, and I will never consent to do it.*
>
> **—Vladimir Nabokov**

Lolita, lounging by the pool. It was the beginning of the end for Humbert Humbert.

Humbert married the mother to be near the bewitching daughter, who combined both an ethereal innocence and a predatory instinct. His wife died in the most perverse manner possible, having discovered his secret journal. Rescuing his little ward from summer camp (Camp Climax), he took her with him to college (stopping at many motels along the way). But someone else was in the picture—someone even sleazier than he, someone whose phantom presence would catch the deceiver in a web of deception, jealousy, and betrayal so dark that insanity, sickness, and murder would be the only possible outcome.

Intriguing? By the time Nabokov had turned his illicit story into a novel in 1955, no American publisher would touch it. Only after the book was published in France (and after the French government outlawed the export of the book) did New York's G.P. Putnam & Sons take a chance on it. The sensational book, though banned in Cincinnati, was a complete smash. *Paths of Glory* (1957) producer James Harris read the proofs and bought the rights from Nabokov (for $150,000 and 15 percent of the net) for his directorial partner, Stanley Kubrick, before the book was a best-seller. When Kubrick finished directing his career-making production of *Spartacus* (1960), he and Harris set about somehow getting *Lolita* produced and getting it by Hollywood's strict Production Code.

The only film company that would consider distributing the hot potato was the Canadian Seven Arts Corporation. After Kubrick had convinced the Code censors that his black comedy would show Humbert as pathetic and more in love than in lust with his nymphet, only two obstacles remained: her tender age must never be alluded to and no hanky-panky noway nohow could be shown. To effect this transformation, Kubrick enlisted Nabokov himself to change his steamy novel to screen satire all in one long flashback, though his first try yielded a four-hundred-page screenplay that would have run seven hours.

Casting was just as tricky. The plum of Humbert was offered up to both Laurence Olivier and Noel Coward, both of whom turned it down. Cary Grant also refused, saying, "I have too much respect for the film industry to do a film like that." But James Mason, the brooding star of many a "weeper" and the tragic hero of *A Star is Born* (1954), took the chance. Kubrick gave him this "inner dimension" to his dapper character during filming: "Smile when you speak your lines and be charming, but all the time be thinking that if anyone dares lay a finger on your suit and soils it, you'll kill them." Mason's veneer of European charm and undercurrent of mania and menace have never been more effective.

Shelley Winters, who had picked up a Best Supporting Actress Oscar for *The Diary of Anne Frank* (1959), was cast as the tender but tacky Charlotte. This Actors' Studio improviser was a handful on the set. As Mason remembered, "No one could ever anticipate her next surprise or wayward whim. She had a jolly good time doing it and she'll be very good in the picture, but it was like playing with some overgrown tarantula."

For Lolita, Kubrick was swamped with letters from mothers offering up their young daughters for the prurient role. Errol Flynn even wrote in tendering the services of his teenage mistress, provided he got to play Humbert. But after auditioning eight hundred wanna-bes, Kubrick saw Sue Lyon, a fourteen-year-old JC Penney catalog model and winner of the Los Angeles Dental Society's Smile of the Year award on *The Loretta Young Show*. She clowned through her first interview with him, sure that she would never get the role, but her mocking manner was just what he wanted for his kittenish and cunning heroine.

The role of Clare Quilty, the debauched playwright who is Humbert's rival for Lolita's affections, was originally a cameo... until Kubrick offered it to comic genius Peter Sellers. The multifaceted Sellers assembled an amazing character, basing his

*ABOVE: Young love is a-callin' as underage bride Caroll Baker beckons to her half-witted hubby Karl Malden in **Baby Doll** (1956). OPPOSITE: Sweet dreams Nabokov style. Humbert Humbert (James Mason) wakes up to find the apple of his eye ripe for a little romp in **Lolita** (1962).*

voice on Kubrick's New York jazz impresario pal, Norman Granz. Quilty's visitation to Humbert in the form of the insinuating college psychiatrist, the Teutonic Doctor Zemf, didn't exist before Sellers improvised it.

In other scenes, the emotionally depressed Sellers began quite morosely until something clicked in him and improvisational ideas would start to flow. In the opening confrontation scene that almost defies explanation, Kubrick recalled that Sellers reached "what can only be described as a state of comic ecstasy." His drunken, hunted Quilty riffs mesmerizingly from playing table tennis to boxing to acting the geriatric cowboy to improvising on the piano to taking a satiric swipe at Kubrick's own *Spartacus* (1960) in a frantic effort to negotiate with the lethal and implacable Humbert.

Kubrick and his cast create both a genuinely heart-wrenching story of one man's twisted, consuming love for a heartless teenage vixen and a biting satire surpassed only by his black-comedy mas-

terpiece two years later, *Dr. Strangelove or: How I Learned to Stop Worrying and Love the Bomb* (1964). Thanks to the lack of sex in the movie (unlike Adrian Lyne's 1996 production starring fourteen-year-old Dominique Swain and a twenty-one-year-old body double), Kubrick snuck his nasty by the Code censors, though the League of Decency's ban on audience members under the age of eighteen could have kept star Lyon from seeing her own work.

Unfortunately, it didn't keep her from Nabokovian fates after a couple of other minor film roles. "My destruction as a person dates from that movie," she once claimed. "I defy any pretty girl who is rocketed into the world of stardom at fifteen in a sex-nymphet role to stay on the level path thereafter." After three marriages by the ripe old age of twenty-five (one to a convicted murderer with whom she first corresponded while he was in prison), this Lolita's path has ended up in a quiet Los Angeles life happily away from the twists and turns of show business.

# Attention: Calling All Dirty Old Men

*No need to be ashamed if you watched certain sections of Lolita more than once. You came to the right place for help. Your first therapy will consist of matching this mob of movie star molesters with the nubile nymphets they become mad for.*

## MAJOR

1. Michael Caine
2. Stacy Keach
3. Karl Malden
4. Ian Holm
5. Robert De Niro
6. Martin Sheen
7. James Mason
8. Keith Carradine
9. Treat Williams
10. Patrick Dewaere
11. Jean Reno
12. Richard Burton
13. Richard Widmark
14. Tom Skerritt
15. Anthony Perkins
16. Fernando Rey
17. Zachary Scott
18. Jeremy Irons
19. Robert Mitchum

## MINOR

A: Laura Dern
B: Juliette Lewis
C: Tatum O'Neal
D: Nastassja Kinski
E: Natalie Portman
F: Lynn Redgrave
G: Coral Browne
H: Ariele Besse
I: Tuesday Weld
J: Jodie Foster
K: Brooke Shields
L: Ann Blyth
M: Drew Barrymore
N: Michelle Johnson
O: Mia Farrow
P: Carole Bouquet
Q: Carroll Baker
R: Dominique Swain
S: Pia Zadora

## MOVIE

a: Dirty old man and pudgy protégé in **Georgy Girl** *(1966)*

b: Occult novelist and hellspawn in **To The Devil—a Daughter** *(1976)*

c: Patron and brothel baby in **Pretty Baby** *(1978)*

d: Humbert and his Lo in **Lolita** *(1996)*

e: Killer and young colt in **Smooth Talk** *(1985)*

f: Child molester and independent orphan in **The Little Girl Who Lives Down the Lane** *(1976)*

g: Lecherous stepdad and psychotic kid in **Secret Ceremony** *(1968)*

h: Wholesome dad and sleazy teen in **Poison Ivy** *(1992)*

I: Old Spaniard and young thing in **That Obscure Object of Desire** *(1977)*

j: A mother's boyfriend and daughter in **Mildred Pierce** *(1945)*

k: Father and daughter in **Butterfly** *(1981)*

l: Cracker and child bride in **Baby Doll** *(1956)*

m: Arsonist and teen vamp in **Pretty Poison** *(1968)*

n: Hitman and waif in **The Professional** *(1995)*

o: Rapist and the daughter of the man who put him away in **Cape Fear** *(1991)*

p: Stepfather and stepdaughter in **Beau Père** *(1981)*

q: Writer Lewis Carroll and his inspiration in **Dream Child** *(1985)*

r: Brit and best friend's daughter in **Blame It on Rio** *(1984)*

s: Eccentric artist and free teen in **Circle of Two** *(1980)*

# FUN AND GAMES WITH GEORGE AND MARTHA

When director Mike Nichols' famous first film, the screen adaptation of Edward Albee's award-winning play *Who's Afraid of Virginia Woolf?*, was being considered for distribution, Hollywood's Production Code administrator Geoffrey Shurlock adamantly refused to give it code approval unless Warner Bros. made its exhibitors sign contracts swearing that no one under the age of eighteen would be admitted without a parent. He had good reasons for slapping this first-ever X rating. Nichols' movie would be "a night of bared souls and misfired lust and spiritual cannibalism" that would "last until dawn when the exorcism is complete," if Warner Bros.' publicity was to be believed. It would highlight the kind of carnage that only married people who know each other's deepest wounds and weaknesses are capable of. And it would star two of the most famous actors of their time who just happened to have that knowledge of each other—Richard Burton and Elizabeth Taylor.

Writer/producer Ernest Lehman (who had adapted scripts for *North by Northwest*, 1959, *West Side Story*, 1961, and *The Sound of Music*, 1965) wanted to "wallop audiences over the head and in the gut" with Albee's sensational story of an aging marriage, corroded by drink and disappointment, between a verbally lethal but washed-out history professor named George and his oversexed, overweight, braying, berating wife, Martha.

Ensconced in the college town of New Carthage (where Martha's father, whom George describes as "a great big white mouse, with little beady red eyes," is the college president), the happy couple staggers home at 2:00 a.m. from a faculty welcoming party and then gets set to personally welcome the new faculty (a polite but studly biology teacher named Nick and his mousy, sterile, moneyed wife, Honey) to their own private battleground. The night (or morning) ahead will unfold unbelievable cruelty, betrayal, humiliation, and lust as the whiskey is poured (count 'em) twenty-two times and sophisticated savagery is cloaked in mind games like "humiliate the host," "hump the host-

> *Elizabeth [Taylor] and I were quite frightened at the beginning, and I'm not joking. We thought we'd have to make a pact. A married couple, if they're intelligent, are bound to indulge in some warfare. However much we tried to be logical and pragmatic and say, 'It's just a job,' we both realized that it would be a life, a life lasting for four months at least, an enormous amount of time.*
>
> **—Richard Burton during the filming of *Who's Afraid of Virginia Woolf?* (1966)**

ess," "get the guests," and "bringing up baby." The unprepared Nick and Honey and those of us truly in the dark are in for what Albee blithely calls "Walpurgisnacht" ("the night that hell opens up").

Sounds fun? The prize roles of George and Martha were first offered to Cary Grant and Ingrid Bergman (Jack Warner wanted big stars to draw the audience into this potentially offensive film), neither of whom had a taste for image suicide and thus turned them down. Albee lobbied for James Mason and Ava Gardner, but the studio brass next pegged Jack Lemmon and Patricia Neal, who also declined (Neal was slated to star as Mrs. Robinson in what was originally to be Broadway wunderkind Mike Nichols' first feature, *The Graduate*, 1967). Bette Davis campaigned like crazy to co-star with Henry Fonda, but Lehman wanted the biggest box-office star in the world, Liz Taylor. So what if she was twenty years too young?

Taylor later said, "The more people who tell me I'm all wrong for it, the more I want to do it." It was when Lehman was at Taylor and Burton's $4,000-a-month rented home in Bel Air securing Taylor's $1,000,000 deal to do the role when the subject of George came up. At the mention of one of his suggestions for leading men, Taylor said, "Put him in it and I won't even go to see it, let alone act in it." Then she pointed across the room to Burton who was listening and announced, "There's your lead-

*Suburban life is great if you can "swing" it. Left to right, Elliot Gould, Natalie Wood, Robert Culp, and Dyan Cannon are of mixed emotions about broadening their friendship in* **Bob & Carol & Ted & Alice** *(1969).*

Let the games (and the humiliation, lechery, confessions, mind-bending, and of course, the drinking) begin. Left to right: Martha (Elizabeth Taylor), Nick (George Segal), George (Richard Burton), and Honey (Sandy Dennis) have only started their Walpurgisnacht in Who's Afraid of Virginia Woolf? (1966).

ing man! My husband!" Her surprised spouse demurred, "Now, wait a minute, love," to which Taylor snapped, "Shut up, darling."

Though Lehman was nervous about Burton's natural machismo coming through, the great actor took a shine to the verbally adept, henpecked role and signed on for a mere $750,000. Burton and Taylor had a two-time Tony Award–winning stage director in mind to bring this play to the screen. Mike Nichols and Burton had met when comedian Nichols was still partnered with Elaine May and Burton was on Broadway in Camelot.

When Patricia Neal had a stroke, The Graduate was postponed and Nichols took the helm of the Albee project. Robert Redford (whom Nichols had directed on Broadway in Barefoot in the Park) passed on playing Nick, and New York actors George Segal and Sandy Dennis were cast as Nick and Honey.

For the exteriors (new to the script thanks to Lehman's seven drafts of adaptation), Nichols had sent production designer Richard Sylbert to visit sixteen colleges across the country. For eleven nights, the cast (including an ironically pregnant Sandy Dennis) suffered the dank New England chill at Smith College in Northampton, Massachusetts. It was there in the dark that Nichols got arguably one of the finest moments on film ever recorded—a colossal nine-and-a-half-minute take of Nick's soul-searing, drunkenly veiled, and uncomfortably autobiographical reminiscence of a boy from his childhood who accidentally shot his mother, killed his father in a car crash, and then remained catatonic in a mental institution.

The outdoor setting also yielded atmospheric gems like the actors' breath rawly visible in the air, creeping fog, and a very natural echo for one of Taylor's inimitable yellings of "Heyyyyyyyy!" Indeed, Taylor, refusing a stunt double, flung herself into the role with such gusto that she knocked herself unconscious on a car in one of her finest moments, the Roadhouse parking lot fight scene ("Snap! The whole marriage just went snap!").

For interiors, Warner Brothers' Burbank stage number eight was closed, even to the likes of Henry Fonda and Joanne Woodward, and guarded by police. Nichols wanted realism and haggled with Lehman over details like why, through twenty-two refills, George never had to go get more ice. He made the studio set the replica of a Williams College professor's ramshackle house. Designer Irene Sharaff was dispatched to universities to observe real people for costume ideas. Prop men were instructed that "the glasses at the bar should be jelly glasses and things that once held pimento cheese. And get some of those terrible green mugs with

no saucers from the dime store." Thomas Mann novels and European posters were scattered about as were old copies of *Mercury, The Partisan Review, The Kenyon Review,* and *The London Observer* (open to the puzzles per Nichols' orders) to work "subliminally" on his audience.

There was nothing subliminal about making a thirty-something glamour queen into a forty-something housefrau. Taylor was told to put on twenty pounds for the role of Martha. The original cinematographer, Harry Stradling, quit when he realized how ugly Nichols wanted to make his star. "We want a certain harshness with Elizabeth," Nichols admitted. "She's so incredibly beautiful anyway, it scares you. So now we show her double chin. We show circles under her eyes. And we also show bitterness." When her stepson, Mike Todd, Jr., visited her and saw her in her extra blubber and salt-and-pepper wig, smoking, swilling, braying, and coughing, Burton kindly claimed that "This is the first time the boy has been really able to look at her and say, 'My God, this is my mother'."

Taylor threw herself into the unglamorous role that required her at makeup a full two hours before her 10:00 a.m. call. Though at first she found herself involuntarily bringing Martha home and appalling Burton with shrewishness and vulgarity, as the weeks wore on, Taylor found herself uncommonly tender with her hubby off the set (having emptied her bile at the soundstage).

For the short scene where Martha wanders into an empty house and screams, "All right, you bastards! I'll give you five minutes," she did special preparation with Southern Comfort high-

balls. After shooting, when she proudly staggered into her famous-for-tippling husband's dressing room, he quipped, "I can only say we don't do things like that at the Old Vic." His time would come. Nichols made the entire cast pull a boozy all-nighter. "We all wanted to see what would happen," said Nichols. "It's easy to say you're tired, and you've been drinking a lot, and it's 5:30 in the morning, but how do you really feel?"

They felt pretty good as the weeks of filming wore on. Burton watched rushes for the first time since his film debut in *The Last Days of Dolwyn* (1949). Nichols was wowed by the professionalism of his potential prima donnas: "The Burtons are on time, they know their lines, and if I make suggestions, Elizabeth can keep in her mind fourteen dialogue changes, twelve floor marks and ten pauses—so the cutter can get the shears and still keep the reality."

Pranks and games were plentiful to break tension on the set. Large sums were bet among the wordsters to see who could define such arcana as "porbeagle," "roup," and "pleach," or identify first lines of novels from *Finnegan's Wake* to *Tropic of Cancer.* Burton

ABOVE: *George Segal discovers this ain't gonna be no simple seduction as Elizabeth Taylor flips in* **Who's Afraid of Virginia Woolf?** *(1966).* OPPOSITE: *Wholesome Roman Polanski takes inter-couple sordidness to the high seas with repressed Hugh Grant and Kristin Scott Thomas, and here crippled Peter Coyote and his smouldering spouse Emanuelle Seigner (Mrs. Polanski to you) in* **Bitter Moon** *(1992).*

(who amazed Segal one day by stopping stock-still in a shaft of sunlight and reciting from Hamlet, then explaining, "No actor should resist a spot like that. Straight from God, you know. Even Jack Warner couldn't supply it.") regularly bet Nichols $5,000 that he couldn't identify pieces of verse the actor would recite. "The money I win from Mike is keeping a godchild of mine going very strongly," he gloated. "Oh so angry is he when he loses."

Nichols may have missed out on the Best Director Oscar that year, but he cemented his screen career (he'd have to wait until the next year to win Best Director for *The Graduate*) and his superb ensemble nailed both Best Actress and Best Supporting Actress. To ensure that kind of quality to the very end, the game-playing director of these game-playing characters had insisted on no less than twelve takes for the riveting final scene of the film (and the last scene to be shot). George and Martha's denouement, amid the shattered pieces of their twisted lives as the sun rises, is somehow tender. As they toddle off to bed, we stagger away from our VCRs. It's been a hell of a night for everyone.

*Love is a Many Splintered Thing, or Get Out Your Therapists*  **63**

# DIVORCE SWEDISH STYLE

*S*ome marriages stay together despite (or perhaps because of) the carnage. Some somehow survive through insanity. But many, many more disintegrate in spite of love. Long before Tammy Wynette warbled it, d-i-v-o-r-c-e originated in ancient Hebrew and Roman cultures. While Judaic law didn't permit a woman to divorce her husband it did allow her to remarry if he divorced her. The progressive Romans on the other hand didn't make marriage a legal formality in the first place. Men and women cohabitated and owned separate property and either could dissolve the partnership with a formal letter.

> **Life is full of messes. Wisdom is in choosing the messes you enjoy the most.**
>
> **—Dorothy Parker**

Only when Christian emperor and famed lawmaker Justinian I came to power did the church try to enforce its view of marriage as an unbreakable contract before the Almighty. Canon law nixed a full split but permitted a separation in cases of infidelity, extreme cruelty, or if a spouse left the Catholic church. An annulment was also legit if it was discovered the marriage didn't adhere to the canon laws on matrimony to begin with.

England's multi-married monarch Henry VIII, who must have foreseen how tedious it would be to execute his unwanted wives, changed the game when he broke with the Roman Catholic church in 1533. Divorce became legal, but each one had to be enacted through the House of Lords, not the courts, which was fine for the rich folks but no one else. In Germany, Martin Luther's own break with Catholicism at around the same time brought Protestant views on divorce as a secular matter. Divorce laws have continued to evolve over the centuries until today, where in the United States in 1990 there were 2.4 million marriages and 1.2 million divorces. Unhappy couples can even relocate to a state with looser laws (like Nevada) when their own states won't legally acknowledge their grounds for divorce.

Let it suffice to say that lots of couples come to that fork in the road but no filmmaker had ever chronicled the bumps along the way to, and beyond it, until Swedish director Ingmar Bergman decided to do a marathon of six fifty-minute episodes on the touchy subject for Swedish television, entitled simply *Scenes from a Marriage* (1973). As the five-time-wived movie legend said, "It took three months to film it, four months to write it, and a lifetime to experience it." And thanks to his incredibly intimate collaboration with actors Liv Ullmann and Erland Josephson, it will be a long time before anyone lucky enough to see the two-hour-and-forty-eight minute film version (Bergman said cutting it was "the hardest thing I've ever had to do"), will ever forget it.

Stunningly beautiful Norwegian actress Liv Ullmann had been first introduced to Bergman by her friend Bibi Andersson and was so impressive she broke the director's exclusively Swedish circle of actors and was cast across from Andersson in the role of the mute in the director's *Persona* (1966). They must have worked closely, for a year after the film Ullmann had a child by Bergman, Linn, and mother and daughter lived with the director for five years. By 1973 the couple had split but, in that wonderful European way, remained great friends and collaborators. Ullmann was between jobs when she called her ex to see if he had anything on the back burner they might shoot together. Bergman immediately began work on a six-part "dialog on marriage" and ended up with a story that followed a seemingly perfect couple—Marianne, a lawyer and a devoted wife, and a boyish-yet-bearish scientist named Johan—down the road to ruin and partial redemption.

Bergman invited Ullmann and a more recent collaborator, Erland Josephson, to his home on an island in the Baltic Sea where they rehearsed for ten days and then, over the next forty-five, sequentially shot one of the most amazing relationship films ever made. The two-hundred-sixteen-page script starts with a scene called "Innocence and Panic," where the seemingly perfect couple and their two daughters are interviewed by a woman's magazine reporter (Ullmann attested, "All the interviewers for the gossip magazines in Sweden are like that, with their little skirts and big belts, always snooping."). They seem gee-shucks happy, but there is something just a little queasily polished and distant about Johan and Marianne admits laughingly that their very lack of problems may be a problem. Things move on to a truly embarrassing dinner with their best friends Katarina (Bibi Andersson) and Peter (Jan Malmsjo), who reveal that behind their own seemingly perfect partnership they loathe one another and are about to divorce.

Scene 2, "The Art of Sweeping Under the Rug," shows us Johan at his lab, where some poetry he wrote is ridiculed by a female colleague whom he seems to know very intimately. He then intimates smugly that he knows someone who loves them—it ain't his wife. At Marianne's workplace, she interviews a divorce-bound older woman who is the very picture of bitterness when she icily admits no love at all for her husband or children. This should give Marianne something to think about, but she goes home and lets her husband berate her for both her sexual awkwardness and her inability to break a weekly social commitment with her parents. (Here, Bergman cut a scene from the shortened film where Marianne discovers she is pregnant and Johan just assumes she will have an abortion.)

Something is rotten in Denmark, or in this case Sweden, and in scene three, "Paula," we find out what it is. Away together in their country house, Johan (Erland Josephson described his character as "a child with genitals, a fabulous combination when it comes to women with maternal feelings") painfully and brutishly confronts his wife with the fact he's been having an affair with a younger woman. He wants to leave Marianne and the kids for her. He's wanted to leave for the past four years. In fact, he's leaving the next morning on a plane for Paris with her for seven or eight months.

A bludgeoned Marianne tries to cope. She tries to understand. She tries to get him to make love with her. She tries to bargain. No

dice. Numbly, they sleep. The next morning, after surreally packing for him (Ullmann really did know a woman who packed for her husband's peccadillos) and then breaking down to almost wrestle him to the floor to keep him from going, the abandoned Marianne phones her best friends for comfort only to find out that they've known all along. The bottom drops out from under the perfect wife and hell yawns to greet her. (In the original, she asks Johan what to tell the housekeeper and he informs her that the maid already walked in on Paula and him making love at home.)

Pretty nasty? Downhill slide ahead? Here's where Bergman stands us on our heads (and makes us love it). In the subsequent scenes, "The Vale of Tears," "The Illiterates," and "In the Middle of the Night in a Dark House Somewhere in the World" which span ten years of reconciliation, insult, seduction, revenge, divorce, battering, and remarriage (for both of them), this couple comes to an honest compatibility and very real feeling for each other as friends and lovers that they never could have had as spouses. The torturous growth on both their parts leaves them, in Bergman's words, with, "all relations in a muddle and their lives incontestably based on a heap of wretched compromises. But somehow they are now citizens of the world of reality in quite a different way from before."

This stuff is as real, and messy, and beautiful as only real life (or excellent film) can be and you have to keep reminding yourself it's not a documentary as often as you have to keep yourself from wincing, laughing, and crying. The acting is superb. As Erland Josephson admitted, "We got to know the characters so well that it became a kind of game to make each episode rather quickly. Liv and I would get up at 5:00 a.m. and prepare our dialogue, and Ingmar was surprised that we knew everything when we came on the set!" The two actors are almost this entire movie. Because it was originally shot on a budget for television they have never-ending yet never-boring closeups revealing the most subtle details of their inner lives.

"We had to make jokes with each other," claims Joesephson, "because we simply couldn't cry all the time."

This was no soap opera; still, when *Scenes from a Marriage* was broadcast in Scandinavia, life in Sweden and Denmark almost came to a standstill. Each week, even traffic cops would abandon their posts to see what was going to become of Johan and Marianne. The divorce rate jumped in Denmark, to which an uneasy Bergman responded, "That's got to be good." But he also grumbled, "I had to have my telephone number changed. People were calling me night and day to discuss their marital problems and seek my advice."

A different kind of approval problem met him when the streamlined series was released as a film in the U.S. Having aired on television in 1973, it was ineligible for Academy Award consideration in 1974, even though Liv Ullmann's performance was so undeniably excellent that she received both the New York Film Critics Circle and National Society of Film Critics awards for best actress. Shortly before the Oscars a group of women took an ad out in the *New York Times* formally requesting the Academy of Motion Picture Arts and Sciences to bend their rule and make Liv eligible for nomination. The undersigned dames were no less than Gena Rowlands, Elizabeth Taylor, Joanne Woodward, Liza Minelli, Sylvia Sydney, Diahann Carroll, Lauren Bacall, Jane Fonda, Glenda Jackson, Ellen Burstyn, Shirley MacLaine, Jennifer Jones, and Ingrid Bergman. Now that's peer pressure.

*If Erland Josephson and Liv Ullmann seem at peace it's because they've been through the wars...known as marriage and divorce in Ingmar Bergman's harrowingly human **Scenes from a Marriage (1973).***

# LUSH LIFE

*I*n one of the many unnervingly honest moments in Mike Figgis' love story with no illusions, *Leaving Las Vegas* (1995), ex-scriptwriter and raging alcoholic Ben Sanderson (Nicolas Cage) admits to a prostitute, "I can't remember if my wife left me because I started drinking, or if I started drinking because my wife left me." One thing he does know is that he's been fired from his Hollywood job, become a pariah in his social circle, drawn out all his cash, paid off his American Express card, burned most of his possessions (including his passport) and stuffed the rest in his car, and driven to Las Vegas with the express purpose of drinking himself to death. He reckons it should take just a few weeks.

> *Drink to me only with thine eyes,*
> *And I will pledge with mine;*
> *Or leave a kiss but in the cup,*
> *And I'll not look for wine.*
> *The thirst that from the soul doth rise*
> *Doth ask a drink divine;*
> *But might I of Jove's nectar sup,*
> *I would not change for thine.*
>
> **—from "To Celia," by Ben Johnson**

Ben has a thirst we've never seen on a movie screen—not Ray Milland in *The Lost Weekend* (1945), not Jack Lemmon in *Days of Wine and Roses* (1962), not even Dudley Moore in *Arthur* (1981) or Albert Finney in *Under the Volcano* (1984). It's so real it's surreal. Watching him buoyantly boogie down a liquor store aisle loading up his cart with every kind of poison under the sun is unnerving (there's that word again). When he almost runs down an unusually classy young streetwalker (Elisabeth Shue, who we've been seeing flashes of in therapy, turning tricks, and being tormented by her

paranoiac Latvian pimp, Uri, played by Julian Sands) at a Las Vegas intersection, it doesn't exactly bode romance. And yet Ben and Sera's meeting is the beginning of one of the most beautiful and heartbreaking love stories ever filmed. There are no background stories to excuse their dysfunction—just courageous mutual acceptance on both their parts as nature takes its course.

John O'Brien, the author of the novel *Leaving Las Vegas*, was an alcoholic who, like Ben, had estranged his wife and told his family, "You are never going to stop me drinking," but unlike Ben, he had some success with his first book. Hollywood wooed him after art dealer Stuart Regen stumbled across the novel at a used-book store. Soon O'Brien had an offer from Mike Figgis for his novel, and was working for *Pretty Woman* (1990) producer Laura Ziskin on a remake of *Days of Wine and Roses*.

Figgis wanted to go back to basics. He had been burned lensing the colossal flop *Mr. Jones* (1993) (a manic-depressive love story between doctor and patient in which studio execs had urged Figgis to downplay the depressive). "I don't ever want to go through the committee system again," confided Figgis. "I don't want to sit down with fifteen thirty-five-year-old ex-agents in suits and have their input on love or sex or death. I have no interest in spending any time with them. As soon as I start thinking about it, I get violent."

To do O'Brien's story, Figgis had to do it the fast and cheap way. Scraping up $3,600,000 for his budget, Figgis had enough dough to shoot in super 16mm (instead of the standard 35mm), which gives the film a beautiful pastel look and required a much smaller camera to stick in actors' faces. Total filming in Los Angeles, Vegas, and Laughlin, Nevada, was limited to a scant four and a half weeks, during which scenes on the strip in Vegas were done amid traffic. "It was a nightmare for the soundman," said Figgis, "but the results were gritty and believable."

The director gave up an office trailer to be able to afford a focus puller. Sting, who had starred in Figgis' first feature, *Stormy Monday* (1988), donated an afternoon of his time—worth about $1.2 million in Figgis' estimation—to record a terrific bluesy-jazz soundtrack of boozy classics in his living room. British fashion designer and former Figgis/BBC documentary subject Vivienne Westwood let Figgis raid her store for his leading lady's clothes. Celebrities like Lou Rawls (as a concerned cabby), Julian Lennon (as a benign biker barkeep), and Richard Lewis and Stephen Weber (as sleazoid agents) all agreed to do cameos on deferred payment.

For his leads, Figgis approached Nicolas Cage, admitting, "I have to say, Nicolas, there is no money. When I say there is no money, I mean you'll probably owe money by the end of the film." Cage, who had just come off three image-improving, upbeat films, *Honeymoon in Vegas* (1992), *Guarding Tess* (1994), and *It Could Happen to You* (1994), was up for a little artistic stretch. It had been a

***It's Ben Sanderson's (Nicolas Cage) birthday, and his new girl Sera (Elisabeth Shue) has given him some nice things... but they're not exactly the will to live. He'll be* Leaving Las Vegas *(1995).***

long time since the actor, known for a level of commitment so intense that it had allowed him to gobble a live cockroach in *Vampire's Kiss* (1989), had jumped off the deep end. According to Cage, the script "left an imprint on my mind that lingered with me. I never looked upon doing the role as a business move; my whole intention was to portray Ben from my soul and if I failed that, then I really was doomed."

There was a dark and rocky road ahead for the actor. "In order to play Ben I knew I had to keep myself in the zone of meditating on death," Cage admitted. He also maintained, "I felt that because it was a short shoot, I could stay on the grill and just get this tunnel vision mode going, and know at the end of the tunnel I would breathe again." Still it was important to him to bring to this potentially wretched character "a sense of being 'up.'" He likened Ben to a man who is going down the river without grabbing for branches so there's no struggle or strain.

To prepare, Cage watched the great drunk movies previously mentioned, then talked to drunks and studied their movements. He also spoke with people who ran programs for alcoholics and claimed, "What I could gather was, the stomach shrinks and contracts like a fist, and the alcohol's like this injection that goes into the body and relaxes the stomach. So the performance really largely comes from the stomach for me."

For the role of Sera, Figgis went out on a limb. Five years earlier, he had met a squeaky-clean ingenue named Elisabeth Shue when she read for *The Hot Spot* (1990), a movie he was going to direct but didn't, and never forgot "something in her eyes." Shue had spent an afternoon "reading through a very tough part that required a complete flip around of personality," Figgis remembered. "It was the virginal girl-next-door who turned out to be a serial killer. It was a tough one to get your chops around, and she did it."

Figgis offered the former Harvard political science major a remarkable role. Sera is honest enough to have no self-delusions in psychotherapy scenes that run throughout the film (for which Figgis was the off-camera therapist), tender enough to care for a character who in Cage's words was "so loathsome that no woman would want to spend five minutes with this man," tough enough to deliver amazingly raunchy lines in a business-like, matter-of-fact tone of voice, and committed enough to straddle Cage, sluicing whiskey down her bared breasts in an effort to literally become the alcohol to which he is so addicted.

Shue spent time interviewing Vegas hookers, learning "that you can turn somebody on and feel nothing for them, nothing. That's how you have power over them. You've been victimized by your past and that means you start to numb out on intimacy." But while Sera's relationship with Ben would be decidedly unsexual almost to the shattering end, sex would be a big part of her role. Nudity was no problem for Shue, who admitted that as an actress she's always had an "exhibitionistic side," but she panicked during blocking rehearsals for a graphic rape scene at the hands of some frat boys. Shue's answer to her fears was to get to know the actors behind the brutes before the scene progressed any further.

Sera and Ben's grab at happiness makes for a film that is hard to watch and impossible not to. With Shue's assured performance of a for-once-realistic "hooker with a heart of gold," with Cage's commitment to self-destruction, and with Figgis' phenomenally quirky, moody, masterful way of telling these two lovers' tragic story,

*Leaving Las Vegas* hit the screens and became the most praised new film since *Pulp Fiction* (1994), winning a Golden Globe Award, an Oscar, four Los Angeles Film Critics Awards, two National Film Critics Awards, and two New York Film Critics Awards.

The story didn't have a happy ending off the screen either. John O'Brien is not lounging poolside fielding his next offer. He's dead.

While the wheels of Tinseltown were turning, O'Brien had allowed his friend David Baerwald to borrow the book's title for a song he was helping write for pop star Sheryl Crow. O'Brien's only condition was that he got some credit for the title. When he heard Crow on television claiming credit for the title for an autobiographical song, he went ballistic.

O'Brien's second novel, *Stripper Lessons*, had fallen through with the Wichita, Kansas, publisher of *Leaving Las Vegas*. He had lost his job at a local coffeehouse and could not afford his apartment. He feared Hollywood would slap a happy ending on his story. And so on April 10, 1994, two weeks before Mike Figgis rolled on his story, John O'Brien sold all his possessions and put a bullet through his thirty-three-year-old brain. All the police found in his apartment was an empty pizza box and an open bottle of vodka. The suicide note is sitting on a shelf in your video store.

*OPPOSITE: Will it be the babe (Jane Wyman) or the bottle for hopeless alcoholic Ray Milland in* **The Lost Weekend** *(1945)? You guess. BELOW: There never was a more sincere (or doomed) kiss, as Elisabeth Shue tries to become the drink Nicolas Cage needs so badly in* **Leaving Las Vegas** *(1995).*

# SCANDAL SHEET, OR WHAT I DID FOR LOVE

*Gadabout playwright Wilson Mizner once called Hollywood "a sewer—with service from the Ritz-Carlton." Right or wrong (who are we kidding?), Tinseltown has developed a scandalous reputation as a Sodom by the Sea, and some of its more illustrious citizens have actually or reputedly gotten themselves into some pretty twisted situations and controversial relationships along its seamy shores. See if you can match up the famous with their supposed infamy.*

## CELEBRITY

1. Mabel Normand

2. Charles Chaplin

3. William Randolph Hearst

4. William Desmond Taylor

5. Thomas Ince

6. Orenthal James Simpson

7. Clara Bow

8. Jean Harlow

9. Lana Turner

10. F.W. Murnau

11. Marlene Dietrich

12. Errol Flynn

13. Frances Farmer

14. Lupe Velez

15. Walter Wanger

16. Stan Laurel

17. Albert Dekker

18. Paul Kelley

19. Rudolph Valentino

20. Roscoe "Fatty" Arbuckle

21. Grace Kelly

22. Roman Polanski

23. Mary Astor

24. Marilyn Monroe

## DIRTY LAUNDRY

**A:** He was acquitted of raping starlet Virginia Rappe with a champagne bottle and causing her subsequent death from peritonitis at the Saint Francis Hotel in San Francisco, but he was banned from the movies for life.

**B:** So jealous was he of Charles Chaplin's affair with his wife, Marion Davies, that when he caught them in the act on his yacht, Oneida, he mistakenly shot producer Thomas Ince (whose birthday party it was), not Chaplin, through the head with a diamond-studded revolver in the ensuing melee.

**C:** During his stormy marriage to a Russian singer, this famous milquetoast is said to have dug a grave and invited her to step into it.

**D:** Her MGM bigwig husband was found nude in front of their full-length bedroom mirror with a .38 pistol by his side. His suicide note read, "Dearest Dear—Unfortunately this is the only way to make good the frightful wrong I have done you, and to wipe out my abject humiliation. I love you—Paul (You understand that last night was only a comedy.)" Supposedly, he was impotent and had tried to make love to her with a dildo the previous night.

**E:** The honeymoon ended when her doctor husband found her blue-bound diary lovingly detailing the sexual athleticism of playwright George S. Kaufman.

**F:** Sexual adventuress extraordinaire, she loved them all, and her "sewing circle" included a gaggle of bisexual actresses, some of whom, like her, liked to wear men's clothes.

**G:** This sexual adventurer almost adventured to jail when charged with the rape of two underage girls, one on his yacht who accused him of violating her through every porthole.

**H:** This former horror star somehow handcuffed himself, stuck syringes in his body, wrote his latest bad reviews on his torso in lipstick, and donned silk lingerie before hanging himself from his shower curtain rod.

**I:** When this screen legend kicked, reports alternately said he was shot by an irate husband, poisoned by a society wife, and died of syphilis. He reputedly married two notorious lesbians and wore a slave bracelet from one of them. At his death, two women attempted suicide in front of his L.A. hospital, another took poison in London, and an elevator boy in Paris was found covered in his clippings. His funeral was attended by phony fascist bodyguards, and two starlets claimed he had intended to marry them. For years a mysterious lady in black brought flowers to his crypt on the anniversary of his demise.

J: This fiery actress left her bite marks on Tarzan husband Johnny Weismuller's chest. Broke by thirty-seven, her boyfriend got her pregnant and told her to get an abortion. She left the following note: "To Harald—May God forgive you and me, too but I prefer to take my life away and our baby's before I bring him with shame or killing him." She had a blowout bash with two girlfriends, then went home and took seventy-five Seconal. Unfortunately her dinner made her sick and she drowned with her head in the toilet.

K: This B movie star was acquitted of the charge of stabbing his ex-wife and her lover to death, though many believe he did it.

L: This zany comedienne was conked into a coma by her intended's lover when she found them in flagrante delicto on the eve of her wedding. Her career ended with news of her cocaine addiction. Later, her chauffeur shot another one of her boyfriends, the son of a Texas oil man. She was named in several divorce cases and died from tuberculosis at the age of thirty-six.

M: This actor almost got away with beating his lover's husband to death when he paid the doctor $500 to say the death was from natural causes.

N: This legendary director died when his limousine crashed. Some say he was going down on his chauffeur at the time. Eleven people showed for his funeral.

O: This major star embroiled herself in a long-term, abusive S&M underworld relationship that ended only when her teenaged daughter stabbed her lover to death in the stomach with a kitchen knife.

P: This producer possessed the key to a private peephole gallery over the beds in the guest rooms of his fabulous Hollywood Hills estate.

Q: This good-time gal was put off limits because of her private sex parties with the entire USC Trojans football team (including young Marion Morrison, a.k.a. John Wayne).

R: Her Philadelphia mainline father stopped in to Confidential tabloid publisher Robert Harrison's office to trash the joint and its occupant.

S: After her failed affair with playwright Clifford Odets and her divorce from actor Lief Erikson, this rebellious actress had a mental breakdown. Arrested after dislocating her studio hairdresser's jaw and running topless down Sunset Boulevard, she signed in at the police station listing her profession as "cocksucker" At her trial she admitted to drinking heavily and taking Benzedrine; when the judge sentenced her to 180 days in jail she screamed, "Have you ever had a broken heart?" and threw an inkpot at his head, then slugged a police matron on the way out.

T: This aptly named producer shot Jennings Lang in the groin when he discovered Lang's affair with his wife, actress Joan Bennett.

U: His wife already murdered by a cult, this director expatriated after he was hauled up on rape charges for having sex with a thirteen-year-old actress during an audition.

V: This playboy director was found neatly dressed with two bullets through his heart. Suspects included lovers Mabel Normand, the twenty-two-year-old screen innocent Mabel Minter, and Minter's mother (also his lover), Charlotte Selby. Investigation revealed that he had vanished from his wife and daughter under another name in New York fourteen years earlier.

W: In July of the year of her drug-overdose death, this star supposedly had a presidential baby aborted at Hollywood's Cedars of Lebanon Hospital.

X: The original chicken hawk, this director married the sixteen-year-old pregnant extra Mildred Harris, who almost died in childbirth and delivered a deformed son who lived three days. He later whisked sixteen-year-old Lita Grey from his Klondike set and took her down to Mexico for a quick marriage. She later divorced him on the grounds that he pressured her to have oral sex and forced her to listen to excerpts of Lady Chatterly's Lover. When she threatened to reveal the names of five other actresses he had slept with during their marriage, he settled for $625,000. Still later, he was sued for paternity by young actress Joan Barry, who had undergone two abortions in his company, and to whom he made love on a bearskin rug when she showed up at his house on Christmas 1942 with a gun in her hand. Despite negative blood tests, the jury found against him.

# Chapter Four

# STEAMING UP THE SCREEN, OR GET OUT YOUR BIRTH CONTROL

*The only film I have ever wanted to make, I will never make, because it is an impossible one. It is a film about love, or of love, or with love. To whisper in the mouth of another, to touch a breast, to imagine and see the body, to caress a shoulder, these things are as difficult to show and hear as horror and illness. I do not know why and it pains me.*

**—Jean-Luc Godard**

*Why don't we d-do it in the road?*

**—John Lennon and Paul McCartney**

*Don't listen to her, Ned! A heavenly (and unusually clothed) Kathleen Turner embroils a horny William Hurt in a plea, a ploy, a plot that will send him straight to hell for his sins in Body Heat (1981).*

Let's get personal. After all, it's just you and a coffee table book. Be honest. You were a little short of breath after crazy crook Jean-Paul Belmondo and free spirit Jean Seberg smoked in bed (literally and figuratively) in Jean-Luc Godard's *Breathless* (1959). You read the Rome society page after seeing Marcello Mastroianni's undercover reporting with Anouk Aimée and Anita Ekberg in Federico Fellini's *La Dolce Vita* (1960). You took music lessons after Oskar Werner, Jeanne Moreau, and Henri Serre showed how much fun playing the triangle could be in Francois Truffaut's *Jules and Jim* (1961).

Let's get really personal. You started keeping cutlery by the bed after Nagisa Oshima's *In the Realm of the Senses* (1976). You invited a girlfriend out to dinner after Susan Sarandon and Catherine Deneuve's vampiric frolic together in *The Hunger*

(1983). You placed an ad for a live-in cook after seeing Sonia Braga dish it out for Marcello Mastroianni in *Gabriela* (1983). You actually practiced saying "Take off your clothes" after Daniel Day-Lewis' success with Lena Olin and Juliette Binoche in *The Unbearable Lightness of Being* (1988). If the answer to at least one of these accusations isn't yes, go back to chapter one, do not pass go, do not collect $200. The following films are hot...hot...hot!

*OPPOSITE: Anita Ekberg is a party girl worthy of a bacchanal in Fellini's look at modern debauchery in* La Dolce Vita *(1960).*
*BELOW: Oskar Werner begins sharing bohemian babe Jeanne Moreau with another man in François Truffaut's* Jules and Jim *(1961).*

# BUILDING UP STEAM

*S*ometimes love means more than holding hands ...much more. No doubt about it: eros has a place in movie romance. Sexually charged films, film relationships, and film performers have been steaming up the screen for a long time. The father of the moving image, photographer Eadward Muybridge, left no place for the Nike logo in his 1870s nude study of *The Running Woman*. By 1897, France's first filmmaker, George Meliés, was tantalizing audiences with *Le Tub*, a short that depicted a certain lady's standing bath in a very low basin.

In the precensored Hollywood of the silent era, not everyone was Mary Pickford. Inspired by a line in a Rudyard Kipling poem about a beautiful bloodsucker, Theodosia Goodman, the slightly frumpy looking daughter of a Cincinnati tailor, was repackaged as Theda Bara (a deliberate anagram for Arab Death) in the film *A Fool There Was* (1915). The "vamp" was born. Sexually aggressive, man-eating (one publicity shot had her hunkered over a skeleton), with alluring dark rings around her great staring eyes, Bara's publicity machine claimed she was born in the shadow of the Sphinx and weaned on the blood of poisonous snakes. As loony as it might seem now, *A Fool There Was* was such a hit that Bara's salary rocketed from $75 to $4,000 a week over three years for forty-odd films (in one of which she wore loosely coiled asps on her breasts).

With sex in the movies, the sex symbol was a hot commodity, especially amid the jazz babies of the Roaring Twenties. Betty Blythe's *Queen of Sheba* (1921) dazzled the gents with a revealing netlike dress of pearls. Rudolph Valentino throbbed female fans as the consummate Latin lover in films like *The Sheik* (1921) and *Blood and Sand* (1922). Comedy king Mack Sennett's slapstick shorts tantalized with bathing beauties that included Colleen Moore (who inspired the word flapper by wearing flapping, unfastened galoshes), Carole Lombard, and Gloria Swanson (who was wisely shacking up with film producer and dynasty patriarch Joe Kennedy). Other directors, such as Erich Von Stroheim, regularly had nudity and sexual material in films like *Blind Husbands* (1919) and *The Devil's Passkey* (1919). It was a wild ride but it didn't last long.

Scandal had already rocked the sports world in 1919 with the Chicago Black Sox fix. The $50,000-a-year job of baseball commissioner went to the honorable Judge Kenesaw Mountain Landis. Likewise, bucktoothed, bat-eared politico Will H. Hays, who had been chairman of the Republican National Committee (during which time some say he had fixed the presidential nomination for Warren Harding), had secured the job of postmaster general (under, whaddayaknow, President Harding) and made a stand against smut being sent through the mail. When silent superstar Roscoe "Fatty" Arbuckle shocked the nation with his alleged lethal rape (with a champagne bottle) of twenty-five-year-old starlet Virginia Rappe during a 1921 Labor Day bash in San Francisco, righteous cries came from all corners of the land to clean up Hollywood. Guess who landed the $100,000-a-year job of tidying up Tinseltown?

> **Will Hays is my Shepherd, I shall not want. He maketh me to lie down in clean postures.**
>
> **—Gene Fowler's biblical poke of fun at the all-powerful Hays' Office**

By 1922, Hays had formed the Motion Picture Producers and Distributors of America, Inc., with movie moguls the likes of Adolph Zukor, Marcus Loew, Carl Laemmle, William Fox, Samuel Goldwyn, and Lewis and Myron Selznick. Escalating state censorship and film distributors' threats to drop the product of studios whose output was too carnal or whose stars were too wild were wake-up calls to producers. As Hays intoned at the association's first press conference, "Above all our duty is to youth. We must have toward that sacred thing, the mind of a child, toward that clean and virgin thing, that unmarked slate—we must have toward that the same responsibility, the same care about the impression made upon it, that the best teacher or the best clergyman, the best teacher of youth would have."

Goodbye, freedom of expression; hello, studio contract morality clauses and undercover investigations of almost every major star in Hollywood. Within a year, Hays had amassed a list of 117 names of stars deemed "unsafe" because of their private lives. As drug and sex scandals saw the light of day and careers were shat-

tered, Hollywood cleaned up its act. Loose-living heroines now died by the guillotine like Madame Du Barry, from stab wounds like Carmen, or from TB like Camille. D.W. Griffith's tale of victimized illegitimacy, *Way Down East* (1920), may have starred the pure Lillian Gish, but Pennsylvania state censors still demanded deletion of Gish's mock marriage, mock honeymoon, pregnancy, and birth, and brought the baby in only just before it expired. Even genius Charles Chaplin's *A Woman of Paris* (1923) got a special American ending where the courtesan played by Edna Purviance went not to another lover (Adolphe Menjou) after her artist beau shoots himself, but selflessly on to run an orphanage.

*OPPOSITE: Betty Blythe and her helmeted paramour seem to foresee with dismay the coming restrictions from the Hays Office censors. ABOVE: Tall, dark, and Latin: matador Rudolph Valentino has a way of slaying the ladies (and that's no bull— just Nita Naldi) in* Blood and Sand *(1922).*

# The Little Engine That Couldn't

etting away with whoopee was possible. Director Ernst Lubitsch had managed it with his aforementioned frothy sex comedies showing chaste singing in boudoir settings. Producer and star Gloria Swanson eked by the censors with W. Somerset Maugham's story in *Sadie Thompson* (1928), about a South Seas floozy who gets raped by a missionary, by inviting Hays himself to lunch, batting her eyelashes, and asking if making the character a lay reformer would make it all better. Notorious "It Girl" ("It" being that indefinable something) Clara Bow—who scored as a seductive ribbon clerk in *It* (1927), promising her employer, "I'll take the snap out of your garters"—also managed to show both flesh and fervor in *Hula* (1928).

Broadway siren of sex Mae West's first screen line (one that she rewrote herself), in the double entendre–titled *Night After Night* (1932), would become emblematic of her deftness with barely cloaked brazenness: to a coat check girl's exclamation of "Goodness, what beautiful diamonds!" West replied in her inimitable nasal tones, "Goodness had nothing to do with it, dearie." Though it was a small role, according to costar George Raft, "Mae West stole everything except the scenery."

West's naughty nimbleness didn't snow all. Sound gave social and religious groups more to be scandalized by and the end of the Great Depression let producers worry about other things besides immediate economic survival. By 1930, with federal censorship looming, Hollywood tried to beat the Hays Office to the punch with an official Production Code that promised "no picture shall be produced which will lower the moral standards of those who see it." In general, the Code laid down the law on scenes of passion, stressing that they "must be treated with an honest acknowledgment of human nature and its normal reactions. Many scenes cannot be presented without arousing dangerous emotions on the part of the immature, the young or the criminal classes." Or, to be more specific, "Excessive and lustful kissing, lustful embraces, suggestive postures and gestures, are not to be shown."

> **They can't censor the gleam in my eye.**
>
> **—Charles Laughton on being told that while starring in *The Barretts of Wimpole Street* (1934) he would not be permitted to show the story's central incestuous relationship.**

Even more specifically, the Code severely restricted any films on taboo topics like adultery ("Adultery must not be explicitly treated, or justified, or presented attractively") and seduction and rape ("They are never the proper subject for comedy"). It outlawed scenes of perversion, miscegenation, white slavery, venereal disease or sexual hygiene, the exposure of children's private parts in bathing scenes, and actual scenes of childbirth (which, "in fact or in silhouette, are never to be presented").

Soon, however, dwindling audiences tempted many studios to let sexuality and other surefire crowd-pleasing vices creep back in. Hays, whose own reputation had been tainted in 1930 when he had been caught bribing civic and religious leaders for their "unbiased" moral assessment of certain films, assuaged the morally avenging call of the Catholic Church's new antismut group, the Legion of Decency, and state censorship boards by establishing the watchdog Production Code Administration in 1934, headed by beloved censorship czar (and ex–altar boy) Joseph I. Breen. The P.C.A. would check everything from costume designs to script drafts to final films in order to ensure adherence to the Code before giving the M.P.P.D.A. seal of approval and distributors wouldn't show films without the sacred seal.

overflowing with froth as they watched an exotic dance had a certain symbolism in *Rain* (1932), the remake of *Sadie Thompson*. While what Samuel Goldwyn termed "a P with an H of G" (a Prostitute with a Heart of Gold) was occasionally O.K.'d, German import Fritz Lang had to add a sewing machine into Joan Bennett's apartment in *Man Hunt* (1941), turning her from seamy into a seamstress. Some directors still relied on their films' punishment of wayward women—Joan Bennett's seductress was stabbed by Edward G. Robinson with scissors in *The Woman in the Window* (1944) and with an ice pick in

Out went Mae West's legendary line from *Belle of the Nineties* (1934), "Is that a gun in your pocket, or are you just glad to see me?" The size of Jean Harlow's apartment in *Wife vs. Secretary* (1936) had to be kept small so that audiences didn't wonder how she supplemented her income. The suggestive white French phone by her bed was even too illicit. In Marlene Dietrich's sexy western, *Destry Rides Again* (1939), a cowpoke was permitted to put money down her dress, but couldn't snort, "Thar's gold in them thar hills!" Even the tasteful Botticelli nude in Twentieth Century Fox's *The Birth of Venus* (1952) had to be cut.

Still, sneaking sex past the Breen Office became something close to a sport among creative film people. Bar patrons' beer mugs

*Scarlet Street* (1945). Alfred Hitchcock got around Cary Grant and Ingrid Bergman's sensual smooch in *Notorious* (1946) exceeding P.C.A. continuous-kiss time limits by interrupting it and starting it all over again. Likewise, Grant and Eva Marie Saint's kiss at the end of North by Northwest (1959) got a certain extra Freudian oomph when the train they were in plunged into a tunnel.

***OPPOSITE: Gloria Swanson in her prime as the seductive Sadie Thompson (1928), which was remade as Rain (1932) with Joan Crawford (above), Dirty Gertie from Harlem U.S.A. (1946) with Gertie LaRue, and Miss Sadie Thompson (1953) with Rita Hayworth.***

Thar may not be "gold in them thar hills" but that does seem to be the territory Jimmy Stewart's surveyin' as Marlene Dietrich looks sultry in Destry Rides Again (1939).

# MEOW!

*Not every heart throbbed to the heartthrobs. Not every bombshell made her target explode with desire.*
*Costars, directors, and critics have doled out some of the most catty comments imaginable to trash an icon's image.*
*See what tacky, shameless, and perhaps accurate things have been said about some of the screen's studs and sirens.*
*You'll have to dig for this dirt, because the names have been scrambled to protect the indecent.*

1. Like kissing Hitler.
   —Tony Curtis on {Lynrami Roonem}

2. They say the best-hung men in Hollywood are {Storfer Rucket} and {Limnot Rebel}. What a shame—it's never the handsome ones. The bigger they are, the homelier.
   —Betty Grable

3. Have you seen {Trober Dorferd} lately? He looks like the proverbial sun-worshipper who's changed into a lizard. That skin! And in close-up yet!
   —Klaus Kinski

4. {Slive Sperley} ended up looking like on the outside what he always was on the inside—an overrated slob.
   —Joan Blondell

5. Doing love scenes with {Kcarl Bagel} in {Enog Whit teh Diwn} was not that romantic. His dentures smelled something awful.
   —Vivien Leigh

6. I was invited to a screening of Samson and Delilah [1949], starring Victor Mature and Hedy Lamarr. Afterwards one of the studio brass asks me how I liked it. I replied, "I never like a movie where the hero's tits are bigger than the heroine's."
   —{Roughoc Ramx}

7. That broad's got a great future behind her.
   —Constance Bennett on {Ralymin Omrone}

8. All my life I wanted to look like {Blazehite Royalt}. Now I find that {Blazehite Royalt} is beginning to look like me.
   —Divine

9. ...{Orcela Blardom} required some artificial help. Before she would go before the cameras, she was famous for yelling out to her costumer, "Bring me my breasts!"
   —Joan Crawford

10. {Rudeya Henburp} is the patron saint of anorexics.
    —Orson Welles

11. Joan Crawford: Hollywood's first case of syphilis.
    —{Teteb Visad}

12. She's like a delicate fawn, but crossed with a Buick.
    —Jack Nicholson on {Sejisca Angel}

13. I can't imagine Rhett Butler chasing you for ten years.
    —David O. Selznick to {Thankiare Burphen}

14. She's silicone from the knees up.
    —George Masters on {Laquer Chewl}

15. A swaggering, tough little slut.
    —Louise Brooks on {Slyhire Pleemt}

16. {Ragy Ropoce} has the longest dick in town, but no ass to push it with.
    —Lupe Velez

17. Katharine Hepburn sounds more and more like Donald Duck.
    —{Bracilee}

18. If Clark [Gable] had one inch less, he'd be the "queen of Hollywood" instead of "the king."
    —{Reolac Boldram}

19. He looks like a dwarf that fell into a vat of pubic hair.
    —Boy George on {Nepric}

20. {Dogile Whan} has a great body, and she's kept it. But she has the face of a chicken, and plus her giggle is what kept her from being sexy or a sex symbol.
    —Andy Warhol

# CHEMISTRY

You can't control a chemical reaction. Some studio stars' chemistry generated heat, even when the stars were clothed and relatively uncompromised. Real life Hollywood Lothario Gary Cooper's legionnaire smoldered ember for ember with Marlene Dietrich's Teutonic tootsie in her first American film, *Morocco* (1930). Barbara Stanwyck was enough of a woman to kindle even Henry Fonda as con artist and prey in *The Lady Eve* (1941). Bacall taught Bogie how to whistle ("You just put your lips together an' blow") in *To Have and Have Not* (1944). A lame Jimmy Stewart and a game Grace Kelly made a New York summer even hotter in *Rear Window* (1954).

One of Hollywood's steamiest love stories had its steam hard-boiled from James M. Cain's 1934 novel, *The Postman Always Rings Twice*. In it, drifter Frank Chambers gets a job at the Twin Oaks, a roadside greasy spoon on the California coast. The restaurant's proprietors are a coarse, elderly Greek named Nick and his much younger, restless wife, Cora. It's animal attraction between Frank and Cora.

In Frank's words, "Except for the shape she really wasn't any raving beauty, but she had a sulky look to her, and her lips stuck out in a way that made me want to mash them in for her." When they're alone Cora begs Frank to bite her. He sinks his teeth "into her lips so deep I could feel the blood spurt in my mouth." The hot stuff gets hotter as Cora and Frank plot to bump Nick off and inherit the Twin Oaks. But "the Postman" (also known as fate) comes back a couple of times to turn things real sour for the sweethearts before it's all over.

With a story this gritty, it took more than a decade (while Cain made it a Broadway play in 1936, the French borrowed the plot for *Le Dernier Tournant* in 1939, and Italian director Luchino Visconti wowed audiences with his own purloined *Ossessione* in 1942) for MGM and the writer of wholesome Hardy family and Dr. Gillespie film fame, Carey Wilson, to sneak a cleaned-up version past the Breen Office. They compensated audiences by pairing two of the hottest actors of their time to play the parts: the dark and dangerous notorious lady's man John Garfield and the sweater girl herself, the luscious Lana Turner.

The script may have been sanitized, but the heat was on. Garfield was quoted once as saying that he had to learn a new skill for every film, yet for this film his task was to make love "and that's something I didn't have to learn." Frank's first encounter with

Cora is one of film romance's most memorable moments. Inside the restaurant, a metal cylinder rolls to Garfield's dusty feet. He stoops to get it and, looking up, first sees a pair of white-pump shod feet, followed by perfect legs up to very short, tight white shorts, preceding a bare tummy and a daring white halter topped by Cora's perfect, pouting face, framed in platinum blonde hair and a white turban. She holds her hand out for the lipstick she dropped and proceeds to languidly touch up those pouty lips that Frank Chambers can never have…or so she thinks.

Hotcha! Hotcha! You can practically see Garfield's (along with every heterosexual audience member's) temperature rise. Oddly enough, all that angelic white (in contrast to Garfield's sexy swarthiness) was director Tay Garnett and writer Wilson's idea. It also boosted the sale of women's shorts considerably. "At the time there was a great problem of getting a story with that much sex past the censors," Garnett remembers. "We figured that dressing Lana in white somehow made everything less sensuous. It was also attractive as hell. And it somehow took a little of the stigma off everything that she did."

Brave new worlds of graphic love began to sally forth in 1959 when the U.S. Supreme Court invalidated a New York law against "cinematographic immorality" (releasing *Lady Chatterley's Lover*, 1955, from legal bondage). The M.P.A.A. ban on "perversion" changed to "prudence, discretion, and moderation." In defiance of the sacred seal, breakthrough films like *The Moon Is Blue* (1953), *The Children's Hour* (1962), *The Pawnbroker* (1965), *Who's Afraid of Virginia Woolf?* (1966), and *Charlie Bubbles* (1968) tackled formerly taboo subjects like virginity, lesbianism, female nudity, profanity, and suggested oral sex, eventually causing the last state censorship board (Maryland) to fall in 1981. Jean Harlow and Clark Gable's stimulating has evolved to Michael Douglas and Sharon Stone's simulating (panties optional) in films like *Basic Instinct* (1992), but some old fogies will say sex was sexier when it was in the mind of the beholder.

*How can someone in so much white be so very bad? But all that hired hand John Garfield sees of boss' wife Lana Turner sure looks good in the* **The Postman Always Rings Twice (1945).**

# Makin' Love Ain't Always Lovely

The movie opens with bluesy jazz accompanying images of strangely flayed, dead-looking but highly sexual reclining nude men painted by Irish artist Francis Bacon. Our first sight of great screen lover Marlon Brando is anguished, disheveled, and unshaved, standing on a bridge and screaming "Fucking God!!!" to the heavens as he's all but drowned out by the din of Parisian traffic. This is where the faint of heart should walk away from Bernardo Bertolucci's infamous screen-steaming, antiromance romance, *Last Tango in Paris* (1973). It's going to be as far away from feel-good Hollywood as you'll ever get.

*Last Tango in Paris* is about an affair between Paul, a forty-five-year-old darker-than-the-darkest-night-souled American (whose French wife, we discover, has just bled herself to death in their bathtub), and Jeanne, a twenty-one-year-old, well-heeled French model (whose fiancé, we discover, is a filmmaker who wants to chronicle her every move). They meet in a capacious, empty apartment that each of them is considering renting in a sleazy pension. Paul's direct, despondent, end-of-his-rope desire is ignited by Jeanne's young, open, prosperous voluptuousness, so without any small talk he takes her up against the apartment wall and they do the wild thing (after which they both slump in separate heaps on the floor).

From that moment on (for three mind- and body-bending days) the apartment (empty except for a mattress, a plain table, and chairs that Paul moves in) will become an arena for exploring the

intimacies and brutalities of sex as well as testing the possibility of a meaningful relationship between two people based on nothing but attraction and the moment. They're in for tough stuff as Paul refuses to learn or give any personal details of his life outside the passion pit. The unvarnished truths that their combination of sex, mind games, and honesty will reveal will lead to madness for one and death for the other.

Who else would you cast for such a role but Marlon Brando, fresh from his beefy, grizzled comeback in *The Godfather* (1972)?

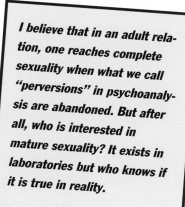

> *I believe that in an adult relation, one reaches complete sexuality when what we call "perversions" in psychoanalysis are abandoned. But after all, who is interested in mature sexuality? It exists in laboratories but who knows if it is true in reality.*
>
> **—Bernardo Bertolucci**

Bertolucci, whose reputation for improvisation was almost as legendary as Brando's, tempted the star with the promise of doing a movie that would be almost entirely improvised and entirely truthful. With Brando's then-wife suing him for custody of their son, Christian, it was just the catharsis he was looking for.

For Jeanne, Bertolucci had originally wanted Dominique Sanda, who had become pregnant. After interviewing more than one hundred actresses, he decided on the cherubic-faced Maria Schneider, whom he termed "Lolita but more perverse." Schneider had left home at fifteen, danced in French stage comedies, been sex symbol Brigitte Bardot's stand-in, and openly embraced a pot-smoking, free-love, bisexual lifestyle. And when Bertolucci asked her to take her clothes off during her screen test, she blithely stripped and, in the director's words, "became much more natural."

Arriving on the set, Brando discovered what would have been disquieting to a more conventional actor. Schneider was also the illegitimate daughter of his old Paris flatmate from 1949, Daniel Gelin. On meeting his leading lady, he took her hand and invited her out for a walk. He felt that they had better get to know each other, considering the extraordinary intimacy of some of the scenes they would be filming. Indeed, they would all be getting to know a lot about each other. Bertolucci and Brando huddled endlessly, talking about psychoanalysis

in between scenes, with Bertolucci shouting at least once at his stars, "You are the embodiment of my prick."

Hard-nosed reality was the watchword of this relentless film. Paul's painfully poignant, postcoital reminiscences about his youth on a farm, his dog, and the cowshit on his shoes that embarrassed him during dates (all of which he later dismisses as fabrications) would seem so real because, as Bertolucci said, "When Brando tells about his childhood, it is his real childhood, with his mother always drunk and the shadow of his virile and violent father somewhere in Nebraska." By the film's end, Bertolucci claimed that Brando vowed never again to make a film so honest. According to the director, Brando "felt raped from the beginning to the end, every day, in every moment. I felt that my whole life, my most intimate things, my children, everything had been yanked out of me."

Brando's performance is so ruthlessly and relentlessly personal that at times it teeters from reality into self-indulgence. In a scene where he confronts his late wife's mother, Brando hit a door so hard with his fist that he had to be taken to the hospital. In a confessional with his wife's pale, smug-looking, funereally arranged corpse, he first attacks her, yelling, "Our marriage was nothing more than a foxhole for you. And all it took for you to get out was a 35¢ razor and a tub full of water." Then he breaks down into heartrending sobs over the corpse, pleading for understanding, capped by a look to heaven that seems to plead for guidance from above. Actually, Brando was looking at a cue card on the ceiling. Indeed, he had his lines (not that he stuck to them) written everywhere, including Schneider's rump, and in a moment where Schneider dances as he sits and plays with his shoe (you guessed it) Brando gave a soleful look of another kind (he had even been limping to avoid smudging his notes).

Schneider had Brando's demons to deal with, too. At their first meeting, Brando set the precarious balance of mentoring and manipulation to their relationship. As they sat in a nearby café, Brando stared at Schneider in silence, finally asking, "Is it difficult for you to look someone in the eye for a long time?" The slightly flummoxed Schneider replied, "Sometimes," to which Brando shushed, "Don't talk, just look me in the eye as hard as you can." She would have to do much more.

In one of their lovemaking sessions (and perhaps the most famous scene in the movie), Paul has Jeanne bring butter from the kitchen and forces her into anal sex while making her repeat a litany of scatological, antisocietal statements. The following day, just after he has tenderly bathed Jeanne's wounds in their tub and dried her off almost paternally, he brutally sets her straight about her romantic love for him: "You want this gold and shining warrior to build a fortress where you can hide in....Well, it won't be long until he'll want you to build a fortress for him....and it's someplace

*Time for a little carnal tenderness (in between psycho-dramatics) for Paul (Marlon Brando) and Jeanne (Maria Schneider) in the very naked* Last Tango in Paris *(1973).*

where he can feel—feel comfortable enough and secure enough so that he can worship in front of the altar of his own prick."

When she insists that she loves him and wants to abandon her hyperkinetic, life-loving boyfriend (wonderfully played by French film star Jean-Pierre Leaud), Paul does even worse. In a scene that is rumored to be real, he tests her love by (bring on the nail clippers) forcing her to stick her fingers up his rear end as he tells her some of the degrading things she'll have to do to prove her love. Eventually she is ready to do all that when the tables turn and the reality they've so carefully constructed explodes.

Then there's the lovemaking. Yes, originally Bertolucci wanted his stars to actually have sex on screen. Brando, however, changed his mind. As he said, "I told [Bertolucci], 'That's impossible. If that happens our sex organs become the centerpiece of the film.'" So, no realism, even if Norman Mailer later lamented that if they had done the deed (and some say they did off-camera) it "would have brought the history of films one huge march closer to the ultimate experience it has promised since its inception—which is to embody real life."

Sex apparently aside, Brando was shocked that he was expected to appear nude and was, in Schneider's words, "very uptight about his weight; he kept pulling curtains whenever he changed clothes." But he also knew that he would be sued if he dropped out of the picture. Mooning a room full of tango dancers when Bertolucci asked him to do "something outlandish" in a surprisingly frolicsome scene later in the film was one thing, but exposing it all? In his first love scene with the unabashedly naked Schneider, the crafty Brando managed to wangle leaving his coat on, emphasizing Paul's alienation. In their subsequent Kama Sutra–style nude scene, Schneider covered for him (so to speak).

According to Brando, he did make one attempt at full frontal nudity. Earlier in the film Paul quips to Jeanne, "That's your happiness and my ha-penis," but the experience was one of the most mortifying moments in his career. "It was such a cold day," Brando explains, "that my penis shrank to the size of a peanut. It simply withered. Because of the cold, my body went into full retreat, and the tension, embarrassment, and stress made it recede even more." For an hour, the naked Brando paced back and forth, "hoping for magic," even talking to his member, while the crew waited, but eventually the gaffers and grips gave up and packed it in.

*Last Tango in Paris* isn't a film for everyone (in Italy it was banned as pornography), but it is a great moment in movie history when its greatest actor and a bold newcomer let it all hang out (almost all, anyway) and showed how cold hot love can be when tempered by the dark night of the human soul.

**Brando broods while Schneider walks into the warped world of their shared love-nest in Last Tango in Paris (1973).**

# SON OF NOIR

*I*t used to be that the only friends a tough guy could count on were a cup of java, a pack of Luckies, and a snub-nosed 38. Today, it's more like a cup of decaf espresso, a self-help book, and a cell-phone. And though we've discarded wing-tips and cement overshoes for Gucci loafers, we still like walking down that sometimes dark, foggy, deserted, slightly sleazy side of the street to that always exotic, erotic, dangerous destination that every human weakness and hunger arrives at— Film Noir.

That French name for Hollywood's most famous film movement began during the fraught forties. As World War II's Holocaust broke all rules of civilization, likewise Noir delved into worlds of fear, suspicion, greed, and betrayal by borrowing from the Depression-era works of writers like Dashiell Hammett, James M. Cain, and Raymond Chandler. Initially, the Production Code Administration nixed the use of these anti-heroic stories of scotch-swilling, cynical Joes and silky voiced, smoldering sirens who led them into a sinister world of crime and passion, but escape is what wartime audiences craved—escape into a world that reflected the moral chaos that many of them felt. Noir also flourished after the war, echoing the hard-boiled cynicism of conquering heros returning stateside to find the world was less than their oyster.

For Hollywood, Noir was just as much of a boon. The hard-boiled detectives and dangerous dames who populated these classics were a boon to any actor or actress who played them and the chemistry between well-matched costars was cool but almost always highly flammable. Sam Spade (Humphrey Bogart) was game for the cunning Brigid O'Shaughnessy (Mary Astor) as he delved into his partner's murder and ended up with a black bird in *The Maltese Falcon* (1941). Detective Philip Marlowe (Dick Powell) rued the day he ever found Ann (Anne Shirley), the ex-con's girl-friend he was paid to hunt down in *Murder My Sweet* (1944). Insurance investigator Walter Neff (Fred MacMurray) took a ride that didn't stop until the cemetery, thanks to tough-cookie, adulter-ess Phyllis Dietrichson (Barbara Stanwyck) in the sizzling *Double Indemnity* (1944).

Humble cashier and amateur painter Christopher Cross (Edward G. Robinson) was led by lust to murder for Kitty March (Joan Bennett) in *Scarlet Street* (1945). Who could resist Rita Hayworth's glove-stripping *Gilda* (1946) as she sang "Blame It On Mame"? Private eye Jeff Bailey (Robert Mitchum) almost took the fall twice for Kathie Moffett (Jane Greer) in *Out of the Past* (1947). Michael O'Hara (Orson Welles) had his final showdown in the hall of mirrors with Elsa Bannister (a blonde Rita Hayworth) in *The Lady from Shanghai* (1948).

Luckily, this chemistry of crime, conscience, and pure carnali-ty has continued through the decades offering other actors just as choice roles. Jack Nicholson not only dazzled audiences in Roman Polanski's *Chinatown* (1974), he steamed the screen with Jessica Lange in the graphic remake of *The Postman Always Rings Twice* (1981) and directed his own sequel to *Chinatown*, *The Two Jakes* (1990). Noir veteran Robert Mitchum resurfaced as the perfect, world-weary Philip Marlowe in *Farewell My Lovely* (1975). Jeff Bridges and Rachel Ward picked up (with a beach coupling to rival *From Here to Eternity*, 1953) where Kirk Douglas and Jane Greer left off in the *Out of the Past* remake, *Against All Odds* (1984).

Mickey Rourke found himself working for the Devil (Robert DeNiro) and daring the censors with chicken blood and *The Cosby Show*'s Lisa Bonet in *Angel Heart* (1987). Femme fatale Theresa Russell wove a web of desire and death for her mates in *Black Widow* (1987). Temptress Rachel Ward struck again with a sleazy husband (Bruce Dern) and a simple-minded boxer lover (Jason Patric) in *After Dark, My Sweet* (1990). Novice private investigator Denzel Washington followed Jennifer Beals into a world of sex and betrayal in *The Devil in a Blue Dress* (1996).

However for many, the most startlingly stylish, sexually charged, and sinister Noir thriller to come down the pike in past decades is Lawrence Kasdan's aptly named *Body Heat* (1981). With its palpable atmosphere of Gulf Coast decadence and its bluesy score, this sultry, sweat-soaked, and serpentine film has enough plot twists, passionate twitches, and career-making performances (big and small) for a fistful of classics.

A twenty-something-year-old Kasdan had been cranking out ad copy in Detroit when his script for the Tracy-Hepburnesque *Continental Divide* (later produced in 1981) caught Hollywood's attention and, more importantly, Steven Spielberg's, who passed the script along to George Lucas, who hired Kasdan to write his second Star Wars feature, *The Empire Strikes Back* (1980). Veteran screenwriter Leigh Brackett's untimely death next gave Kasdan a shot at writing Spielberg's *The Raiders of the Lost Ark* (1981). Kasdan then wrote a new script based on his observations of the get-rich-quick-attitude, the disappointed idealism, and the failed promise of plenty he saw in his own baby boomer generation. It followed a charming, lazy, unprincipled, studly lawyer named Ned Racine who makes the mistake of his callow life one sweltering summer night when he begins a torrid affair with a local beauty, Matty Walker. The problem is that Matty is married to a much older, stinkingly rich, frequently absent, real estate developer. As the fervor of their affair escalates, Ned finds himself plotting with Matty to kill her husband and inherit his cash…until things start getting strange enough to make both him and us question just who is plotting against whom.

Armed with incredible credentials and a hell of a script, the thirty-two-year-old writer made a hell of a deal with Twentieth Century Fox president, Alan Ladd Jr., to direct his own picture.

> **When you show how you make love, you show how you feel about yourself —how you feel about your body. Your whole world is there.**
>
> **—Kathleen Turner as Kathleen Turner**

When Ladd left Fox and Kasdan wanted to cast unknowns from "the tremendous log jam of talented actors," Fox pulled out. Luckily, Ladd brought the project on board with his newly formed production company. For his leading man, Kasdan looked to New York actor and film neophyte William Hurt, whose hunky, WASP good looks, intellectual intensity, and off-beat vocal rhythms made his power, in Kasdan's words, "both raw and refined."

Hurt, who had described himself as a character man trapped in a leading man's body, and whose love of acting admittedly included the emotional pain and challenge of exposing his innermost wounds, claimed he was attracted to the role of Ned "because I recognized so much of his personal anguish. He's gone through school, trained, struggled to build a practice, yet he feels unfulfilled. His predicament is not as uncommon as some might expect." Hurt found affinity with Kasdan for his "great joy in passing on ideas." "Ideas are like buses. Directors are like a Port Authority of ideas," the actor somewhat cerebrally added.

Matty was another matter. Star of Broadway's *Gemini* and daytime TV's *The Doctors*, smokey-voiced, twenty-six-year-old Kathleen Turner had never acted in a feature film role. In fact, *Body Heat*'s New York casting agent told her she was "totally wrong for the part." But Turner felt "it was one of those scripts that make absolute sense. I knew the rhythms already. It clicked immediately. I wanted to play Matty more than any other character I had ever read."

While in Los Angeles to audition for the role of a lady wrestler for *All the Marbles* (1981), Turner and agent/boyfriend David Guc not only wangled an audition for *Body Heat*'s West Coast casting agent, Wally Nicita, they also managed to sneak a peek at the entire script (Kasdan had only been giving actors pages so they wouldn't try to play the whole role in the audition). An impressed Nicita set up a reading for Kasdan (Matty's confession about her past as a drug addict in Chicago). Turner walked into Kasdan's office, lit a cigarette, and stretched out on the sofa ("I was desperately trying to appear completely in control the way Matty would be."). Breaking the silence after her reading, an amazed Kasdan said, "I didn't think I would ever hear that scene read the way I hear it. Let's do it."

Still, the Ladd Company brass were nervous about staking so much on an absolute beginner. Apparently they set up an in-person reading with Turner in their pristine, white decorated offices. When Paula Weinstein asked Turner about her role of Nola Aldrich on *The Doctors*, the actress responded that she liked the character because she got to play drunk a lot. She demonstrated. "I slurred a few words, struggled out of my chair and threw my script down on the table," Turner remembered. "The ashtray went sailing off the table with butts and ashes flying all over Alan Ladd Jr.'s beautiful white decor." The resulting embarrassment, vulnera-

bility, and hilarity , which allowed everyone present to dispel their tension, are what Turner is convinced landed her the role.

The chemistry between Turner and Hurt was undeniable, though early dinners with the former theology student gave Turner pause. "I mean it got a little scary sometimes," she admitted, "like spending a whole evening talking about your preferred mode of death. He said he would like to be sucked up by a jet engine and immediately atomized." But flaky Hurt was flakeless on the set. Love scenes were reserved for the final weeks of shooting. Turner told Kasdan, "I don't want to be the token nude." Kasdan, in turn, convinced Hurt to get just as naked and told his actors in step-by-step detail each shot they'd be taking for every love scene ahead of time, standing by his word as to exactly how much the camera would see. The camera would see a lot. Turner's costume later would be cited by critics as alternately William Hurt and a cigarette, and just a cigarette.

The first love scene where Ned follows Matty home to "listen to her wind chimes," experiences her kiss only to be locked out of the house, and then throws a chair through the porch window and takes Matty on the living room carpet, needed trust and preparation. Turner maintained that you can't get too carried away in a love scene without rolling out of frame and that even though her body was responding while her head was saying, "O.K., now the camera is there and I have to kiss him at three-quarters," she found the word "CUT!" a good cold shower. To break the tension of lying naked while technicians adjusted lighting equipment, Turner and Hurt competed to see who could remember the most Shakespearian sonnets.

Cunningly directed sex and suspense, languid cinematography, a mind-blowing ending, and riveting supporting performances by Mickey Rourke and Ted Danson as a warm-hearted arsonist and a twinkle-toed prosecuting attorney make *Body Heat* (1981) Film Noir at its very best. And though its heat began unfounded rumors of Turner's affair with both her director and costar, it launched her and Hurt into the realm of sex-symbol superstars. Turner may have woken in the middle of the night during filming to lie in bed, "scared to death that people were going to see one of those smoldering looks and start giggling," but giggling wasn't the sound coming from most audiences.

*Sometimes a gun is more than a gun. Sleazy Florida lawyer Ned Racine (William Hurt) workin' up a little* **Body Heat** *(1981) with wealthy Matty Walker (Kathleen Turner).*

# TURNABOUT IS FOREPLAY

*P*leasebabypleasebabypleasebabypleasebabypleas Spike Lee addressed himself to matters of race in films like *Do the Right Thing* (1989), *Jungle Fever* (1991), *Malcolm X* (1992), and *Clockers* (1995), he attacked sexual politics head-on in a very, very sexy film. *She's Gotta Have It* (1986), the up-front title of Lee's first feature (and a play on the vintage Hollywood sexpot film title, *The Girl Can't Help It*, 1956), doesn't pull any punches, not unlike its director. It was shot in a mere eleven (count 'em, eleven) sweltering July days in Brooklyn. Its budget was so slim ($60,000 in actual cash) that the developing lab had threatened to destroy shot film for lack of payment, and before each shooting day, production supervisor Monty Ross would first check back at Lee's Forty Acres and a Mule production office to see if any new checks had come in. Yet the final result was so fresh, funny, insightful, and hot-hot-hot that it won its twenty-nine-year-old director the coveted Prix de Jeunesse at the Cannes Film Festival.

Necessity, that mother, had given birth to invention. The summer before Cannes, Spike was desperate. After eight aborted weeks of preproduction on a film about a bicycle messenger, he had found himself almost out of funds but hell-bent on making some kind of film (as evidenced by his journal: "Too, too often black people have had to rely on Hollywood to tell our stories. I'm determined to change that even if it's only in a small way. We shouldn't have to rely on the Spielbergs to define our existence"). His $18,000 grant from the New York State Council on the Arts was intact, but when *Messenger* rolled out so did his $20,000 grant from the American Film Institute. Now he needed to make a "movie that would have very few characters, almost no locations," Lee wrote in his journal, "but—and this is important—could still be a commer-

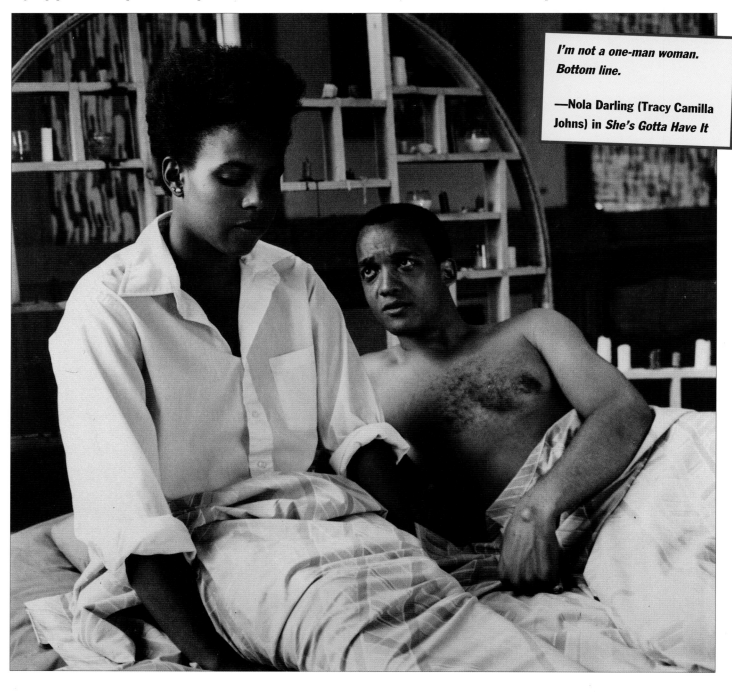

I'm not a one-man woman. Bottom line.

—Nola Darling (Tracy Camilla Johns) in *She's Gotta Have It*

cial film, a good film. So I came up with a script that could be done as cheaply as possible."

It was the kind of story that had rarely been attempted (without heaps of moral retribution) in Hollywood. "I have a lot of friends who like to talk about all the women they have," Lee explained, "but let a woman even think about having more than one man and they go berserk." His idea was sort of a romantic *Rashomon* (1950), shot in black and white with all parties interacting as well as intimately addressing the camera. In the center of the story is Nola Darling (Tracy Camilla Johns), a young African-American graphic artist whose unabashed appetite for sex and refusal to conform to society's norms ("I consider myself normal, whatever that means—some people call me a freak") has created a thorny, horny, hilarious ménage à quatre.

There's her bicycle messenger, Mars Blackmon (the deadpan Lee himself), who makes her laugh ("All men want freaks, we just don't want 'em for a wife"). There's Greer Childs (John Canada Terrell), her hunky but oh-so-narcissistic male model ("I was the best thing that ever happened to Nola. When we walked down the street, heads turned"). And there's Jamie Overstreet (Tommy Redmond Hicks), the regular Joe she loves, who just wants her to settle down with him ("I was just minding my own business waiting for the 41 bus when you walked by. I know it sounds corny but if I didn't follow you I might never see you again"). We also get the perspective of Nola's overly attentive, lesbian best friend, Opal Gilstrap (Raye Dowell), and Nola's understanding therapist, Dr. Jamison (Epatha Merkerson).

Homegrown is the word for this movie. The cast and crew from Spike's New York University film school thesis, *Joe's Bed-Stuy Barbershop: We Cut Heads*, all worked on *She's Gotta Have It* for deferred payment. His sister Joie contributed as Nola's exasperated ex-roommate Glorinda Bradford, who has tired of Nola's parade of men. Spike's father, Bill Lee (who also composed and played the film's bluesy score), subbed as Nola's father. Spike's grandmother, Zimmie Shelton (who actually had a crazy great-uncle named Mars), had even invested $4,000 of her life savings into the production.

To prepare for the film, Lee and female friends Mindy Goldman, Tracey Willard, and Barbara Russell had prepared an A.S.S. (Advanced Sexual Syndrome) survey. Approximately thirty-five women that they knew were taped responding to a list of forty questions on female sexual attitudes and experiences. Some examples: #5—"Is making love different than sex? Why if so?";

**OPPOSITE: Jamie just can't seem to satisfy his wandering woman in Spike Lee's She's Gotta Have It (1986). ABOVE: Three-timin' it. Clockwise: The desirable Nola (Tracy Camilla Johns), the straight-laced Jamie (Tommy Redmond Hicks), the out-there Mars (Spike Lee), and the narcissistic Greer (John Canada Terrell).**

#11—"When you gotta have it, how do you get it?"; #19—"Do you feel all men are basically dogs?"; #27—"Approximately how many men have you had? Any regrets?"; #29—"Describe your most memorable encounter."; #36—"Do you care if people put labels on you—loose, etc?"; and #40—"What part of your body is the money?"

"We found women who were virgins," he exclaimed, "women who'd been to bed with a hundred men, even women who'd been in the middle. It really helped free up my imagination." Lee also made notes to himself in his journal to study up on black women's literature: "*Sula, Bluest Eye, Song of Solomon, Their Eyes Were Watching God, The Color Purple,* and some Sonia Sanchez stuff, too." For handling a documentary style he would watch Woody Allen's *Zelig* (1983) to "see what I see and what I shouldn't do."

Lee also wanted to correct a few racial stereotypes. He made Jamie Overstreet so square that he seemed like Ozzie Nelson with a sex drive. Greer Childs was as effete as any white snob. To get away from the media's version of the "beautiful black woman: the classic octoroon-quadroon-mulatto-Vanity-Appollonia look," he cast a gorgeous but totally down-to-earth, distinctly afro-headed and African-looking Tracy Camilla Johns as Nola. For the smart-mouthed Mars, with his homeboy attire (including sneakers that he even wears in bed), Lee's own character "was in direct response to the Bernard Goetz thing, because not every black kid wearing a Kangol [hat] and high-top sneakers with fat laces is going to rob you."

The relationship between the four central characters is truly hilarious as the men compete against each other, bitch about each other, and almost drive the divine Nola crazy in the process. You don't want to miss the Thanksgiving dinner where Nola finally brings them all together for a truly surreal evening. Funnier still is an earlier montage of men (referred to as "dogs" in the script) from Nola's past and the outrageous lines they have tried to ply her with. Here's the list. Feel free to try them out.

Dog #1: Slim, you so fine I'd drink a tub of your bath water.

Dog #2: Congress has just approved me to give you my heat-and-moisture-seeking MX missile.

Dog #3: I wanna rock ya world.

Dog #4: If I was you, I'm the kind of guy you'd want to take home to meet your mother. Don't you agree?

Dog #5: Baby, it's got to be you and me.

Dog #6: You may not realize this but you are sending out strong vibes tonight. May I continue? You're lonely, you're alone, you're sad, you're confused, you're horny. You need a man like me to understand you, to hold you, to caress you, to love you. You need me. What's your phone number?

Dog #7: I know I only saw you for the first time in my life one minute ago but I love you.

Dog #8: I got my B.A. from Moorehouse, my M.B.A. from Harvard. I own a new BMW 318i, I make fifty-three thou a year after taxes and I want you to want me.

Dog #9: Did you know I'm related to Michael Jackson on my mother's side of the family, and Prince on my father's? No lie. We can call them up right now.

Dog #10: Baby, I got plenty of what you need. Ten throbbing inches of USDA government-inspected prime-cut grade-A Tubesteak!

Finally, the M.P.A.A. wanted to give Lee's film an X rating because it was "saturated with sex." It wasn't just saturated; it was overflowing. And "steamy" was all too appropriate since in the Brooklyn loft that served as Nola's apartment (with an altarlike bed surrounded by dozens of candles) the windows wouldn't open, sending temperatures soaring up to 100°F (38°C) without the lights on. In his journal Lee had mused, "The sex scenes have to be interesting or this whole thing will be monotonous—just people boning and we don't want that."

He had originally envisioned shooting some sex scenes twice: "Nola says, 'He didn't take enough time,' and we shoot it at high speed. The man says, 'I really gave it to her,' slow motion. Both are describing the same act." Some shots were lost in his three cuts to change his X to an R—such as the scene where we see Nola doing it doggie-style with all three of her lovers in rapid succession. Some shots remained, like the extreme close-up of Mars tonguing Nola's breast ("This is one of my favorite shots in the film. This is the world-famous, slow-motion, Mount Kilimanjaro nipple shot."). It's every bit as sensual as the ice cube treatment Lee gives Rosie Perez in *Do the Right Thing* (1989).

*She's Gotta Have It* is sex with a social conscience and an exciting look at the blastoff of one of today's hottest filmmakers. As to how Nola resolves her dilemma (what decision Lee made after the A.S.S. survey, the reading, and the eleven crazed days of shooting), let's just say You Gotta Watch It. And for the uncensored at heart, the unexpurgated version is available on laser disc.

**Annabella Sciorra and Wesley Snipes don't need furniture to get steamy in Lee's Jungle Fever (1991).**

# WITH FIFTEEN PEOPLE ON THE SET?!?!

*Love scenes look easy, but in fact they're among the hardest of scenes to pull off. An Officer and a Gentleman (1982) director Taylor Hackford likened it to "catching lightning in a bottle—and just as hard to achieve." As Sea of Love (1989) director Harold Becker admits, "The audience has to feel this is totally spontaneous. And yet it never is. The art is to make it appear as if [the eroticism] just happened that way. You don't want the audience to ever feel, even for a second, that it was all engineered. Even though it was." See if you can match up the behind-the-scenes peek at the mechanics of the steamy scene with the actors involved and the movie it comes from.*

## BEHIND THE STEAM

**1.** These two co-stars made no bones about their dislike for each other on the set. Yet when they got their clothes off and the director piped in Stevie Wonder and Van Morrison music...va-va-va-voom. As the male of the duo said, "Tension is no bad thing. You can use it to get the relationship onscreen very urgent and edgy."

> Suddenly you wind up in bed with a guy on top of you that you wouldn't want to share a cab with.
>
> —Candice Bergen

**2.** This leading man was cold for his ladylike lady until she started swearing like a sailor, telling him, "If I were you, I'd tell that bitch to go back to England and fuck herself!"

**3.** This starlet was offered a $5,000 bonus by producer Hal Wallis if she could give her retiring and gentlemanly costar an erection during their love scene. She then probed his mouth so deeply with her tongue that as their lips parted his partial bridge flew out of his mouth at her.

**4.** In the midst of one of the most famous screen clinches in history, this movie star yawned, looked up at his director, and said, "What time is it, Mike? I'm hungry."

**5.** To keep her mouth fresh this sex symbol chewed gum and wadded it next to her teeth while she puckered up. But this macho hunk, who once said he had to imagine "a medium-rare Kansas City steak" to put any power in his pucker, kissed her too forcefully, and when their mouths parted, a string of gum slung between them. Said she, "From then on I gargled."

**6.** Rumor has it that this much-publicized erotica was the ultimate love scene, i.e., real.

**7.** This steamless love scene was such a flop that its star turned down the lead in American Gigolo (1980).

**8.** On the set of this one the director stood to the side and shouted instructions and encouragement "like a demented cheerleader."

**9.** After one take was ruined when they fell off the divan and another when her dress caught on fire and he doused her with a bucket of water, this screen siren took her nervous, young leading man home with her, plied him with champagne, and taught him a thing or two. The next day, to crack his last resistance, she covered his face with kisses on camera.

**10.** Rumor has it that Louis B. Mayer monkeyed with the soundtrack for this loathed leading man's first talkie, making his murmured "I love yous" so high and squeaky that audiences booed him out of the movies.

**11.** During a notorious wrangle in the back of a limo, this fiery actress shouted at her flustered costar, "Pull yourself together. I'm the one without any clothes on."

**12.** The fact that "we had to make love while circling around the room in three different states of undress" left this actress with a "distinct feeling of motion sickness."

**13.** These two neophytes were allowed to keep their underwear on for their steamy scene and got two days of private rehearsal away from the crew with their director.

**14.** This sensational love scene required six thousand feet (1,829m) of film detailing its two stars' oral sex, and the director employed a body double for some of the more revealing moments, but he only used the most potent one hundred feet (30.5m) of film.

**15.** This screen duo was stopped in midkiss by their director, who admonished, "No, I really want your nose on the right side of her nose, because on the left side you're blocking the light."

**16.** Their three-minute pucker is the longest kiss ever recorded in a movie.

**17.** For this romance, he taught her "to kiss like an adolescent on the first date" because "the camera will multiply it a hundred times."

**18.** Their legendary censor-shocking lovemaking on the beach was a little less romantic than it looked. Said he, "The water was freezing, and sand got in our hair, our mouths, and up inside the swimsuits."

**19.** Her notorious hot-tub scene gave her an infection.

**20.** In one of Hollywood's most romantic movies, she complained that he was spitting on her while he spouted words of love, so in their love scenes they were moved a few feet further apart.

**21.** This self-confessed libertine actually asked for little pillows to be placed all over her bedmate's body so she wouldn't actually touch him.

## THE DREAM TEAM

**A:** Greta Garbo and Robert Taylor in Camille *(1937)*

**B:** Michelle Pfeiffer and Mel Gibson in Tequila Sunrise *(1988)*

**C:** Errol Flynn and Olivia de Havilland in The Adventures of Robin Hood *(1938)*

**D:** Vivien Leigh and Clark Gable in Gone With the Wind *(1939)*

**E:** Michael Douglas and Glenn Close in Fatal Attraction *(1987)*

**F:** Meg Tilly and Colin Firth in Valmont *(1989)*

**G:** Mickey Rourke and Carré Otis in Wild Orchid *(1990)*

**H:** Susan Sarandon and Catherine Deneuve in The Hunger *(1983)*

**I:** John Travolta and Lily Tomlin in Moment by Moment *(1978)*

**J:** Humphrey Bogart and Ingrid Bergman in Casablanca *(1942)*

**K:** Sean Young and Kevin Costner in No Way Out *(1987)*

**L:** Corinne Calvet and Joseph Cotten in Peking Express *(1951)*

**M:** Lana Turner and Clark Gable in Homecoming *(1948)*

**N:** Jon Voight and Jane Fonda in Coming Home *(1978)*

**O:** Regis Toomey and Jane Wyman in You're in the Army Now *(1941)*

**P:** Burt Lancaster and Deborah Kerr in From Here to Eternity *(1953)*

**Q:** Richard Gere and Debra Winger in An Officer and a Gentleman *(1982)*

**R:** Laurence Olivier and Merle Oberon in Wuthering Heights *(1939)*

**S:** Ryan O'Neal and Ali MacGraw in Love Story *(1970)*

**T:** John Gilbert and Catherine Dale Owen in His Glorious Night *(1929)*

**U:** Shelley Winters and Michael Caine in Alfie *(1966)*

# Chapter Five

# THE EYE OF THE BEHOLDER, OR GET OUT YOUR PRECONCEPTIONS

*Le coeur a ses raisons que la raison ne connait point. [The heart has its reasons which reason knows nothing of.]*

—Blaise Pascal

*We know that Art is not truth. Art is a lie that makes us realize truth, at least the truth that is given us to understand.*

—Pablo Picasso

Mrs. Robinson (Anne Bancroft) just wants to give Benjamin (Dustin Hoffman) a leg up in life. Why does he look so...uncomfortable? A vintage moment from Mike Nichols' masterpiece of modern love, The Graduate (1962).

*J*ust who gets to be in a love story? What qualifies as falling in love? Is a love story something that's supposed to touch us, make us laugh, make us hot, or make us think? Can it do all of that at the same time? What happens when the couple in question is of the same sex or a different race? Can a love story tackle controversial societal issues? Where does divine leave off and deviant begin? Are some couples just too weird for an audience to accept? Is love ever in bad taste? Can we ever really go back to plain old-fashioned boy-meets-girl again?

Imagine conservative studio honcho Moe Gull being asked to green-light the following contemporary projects fifty years ago during Hollywood's golden age. Here's the windup...and the pitch:

"It's a classic. The boy is an I.R.A. terrorist with a heart. The girl is the feisty, chanteuse lover of the English soldier he held hostage and befriended before he helped kill him. Remorseful, the Irishman looks her up and they fall in love. But she's black and not exactly a she." "NEXT!" "You're right, M.G. Here's a peach of a comedy. This funny, affluent, New York couple adopt this way-cute, megabright kid. Dad becomes determined to learn about his son's biological mother. He tracks her down. She's a single babe who's totally lovable but not so classy, so he wants to help refine her and match her up. Along the way they fall in love. Did I mention that she's a hooker with a weird, squeaky voice?" "NEXT!!" "How about this import? She's a fat, homely kleptomaniac, the unemployed daughter of a corrupt Australian politico. Her best friend is a paraplegic, but she meets this South African swimmer who needs to get married.

Did I mention that she's into Abba?" "NEXT!!!" "Okay! Right! How about she falls in love with the hitman her husband contracted to kill her?" "NEXT!!!!" "Absolutely. He's a guy drinking himself to death and she's like this guardian angel. Did I mention she's a hooker, too, and that he's impotent?" "NEXT!!!!!" "I see what you mean. They're kids in love but both his parents are men. Well, actually one is a female impersonator." "NEXT!!!!!!" "Why didn't I see that? They're both writers and in love but he's gay so they don't have sex." "NEXT!!!!!!!" "Agreed, but this is solid gold. She's a nun. He's a redneck, death-row inmate in for raping and killing two teenagers." "MISS JONES!!!!!!!"

Luckily this isn't the good old days, and the envelope for a great movie love story expands a little every year. As "a million points of light" have illuminated the "beautiful mosaic" that has been brought "out of the closet" and into "the global village," the blonde and the beautiful have retreated ever farther into TV land to make way for a much realer cast of romantic characters on the big screen.

Nor has love been the sanitized sanctuary of porch swings, sock hops, and moonlit kisses. The sixties may have given us Frankie and Annette in *Beach Blanket Bingo* (1965), but it also put *Bob & Carol & Ted & Alice* (1969) in bed with each other. Julie Andrews may have fulsomely embodied working-class purity and moral freedom as she warbled on a hillside in *The Sound of Music* (1965), but Marlon Brando embodied upper-class decadence and sexual repression as he warped himself for the lust of a junior officer in *Reflections in a Golden Eye* (1967).

Movie by movie, love stories have gone where cameras feared to tread. Lindsay Anderson's *This Sporting Life* (1963) took a brutal look at love and class-consciousness in England. Jan Kadar and Elmar Klos examined the fine line between love and collaboration in Nazi-occupied Czechoslovakia in *The Shop on Main Street* (1965). Hiroshi Teshigahara's *Woman in the Dunes* (1964) bugged out an entomologist in a desert world of love and survival. Sydney Pollack's *They Shoot Horses, Don't They?* (1969) pitted sweethearts against the heartless prism of the Great Depression.

Perhaps most importantly, by the sixties a new generation was being shown coming to terms with this thing called love, whether it was Marcello Mastroianni in *La Dolce Vita* (1960), Macha Meril in *A Married Woman* (1964), Hana Brejchova in *Loves of a Blonde* (1965), Lynn Redgrave in *Georgy Girl* (1966), or Dustin Hoffman and Katharine Ross in a little film called *The Graduate* (1967).

**OPPOSITE TOP: War has a poignant way of making enemies into allies in The Shop on Main Street (1965). OPPOSITE BOTTOM: Stephen Rea and the beauteous Jaye Davidson are just as marvelously "mismatched" in The Crying Game (1992). BELOW: Duckling-into-swan Toni Collette and Bill Hunter also proved the nay-sayers wrong in Muriel's Wedding (1994).**

# LESSONS IN LOVE AND ANARCHY

*L*iterally on the heels of his iconoclastic, X-branded triumphant attack on marriage with *Who's Afraid of Virginia Woolf?* (1966), Mike Nichols made what may be the quintessential sixties love story, the highest-grossing film of its day after *Gone With the Wind* (1939) and *The Sound of Music*—the one, the only, *The Graduate*. Charles Webb's 1963 novel was purchased by producer Lawrence Turman for $1,000 of his own money after reading a review of it in the *New York Times*. By 1967, producer Joe Levine had raised the $3.5 million needed for the boy wonder, director Mike Nichols, to make it.

Buck Henry and Calder Willingham's script chronicles the struggles of recent eastern-college grad Benjamin Braddock, who returns to the bosom of his fat-cat, Los Angeles family. The responsible Ben just wants to get his head together (he is "worried about his future") but his parents have arranged a party in his honor. At it, his parents' friends grab, tousle, maul, muss, hug, back-slap, commandeer, and corner the newspaper-editing, scholarship-getting, track-star golden boy

(with such sage words as "I just want to say one word to you—PLASTICS!"), but one old family friend takes a particular interest.

Mrs. Robinson, Ben's father's law partner's world-weary and sexy wife, marshals him to drive her home in his Alfa Romeo. She has him escort her into her empty house and accompany her to the sun porch. Then with the confidence and detachment of a sexual Machiavelli, she plies him with hard liquor and soft jazz and informs him that her husband won't be back until very, very late. A shocked and overly polite Ben gets the message ("Mrs. Robinson, you're trying to seduce me.... aren't you?"), which his hostess languidly denies. However, before he can awkwardly extricate himself, she manipulates him into dutifully unzipping her dress and then bringing her purse to a bedroom where, naked, she offers herself to him either now or at his convenience.

It's a dull summer in L.A.'s sprawling, sunny suburbs and eventually the alienated, virginal Ben takes Mrs. Robinson up on her offer. They hilariously rendezvous at the Taft Hotel, and for the next several weeks, Ben's world blurs into the carnal bliss of days swimming in his family's pool and nights spent stroking in Mrs. Robinson's detached but delectable waters. Then the bomb drops. After much pressure from his parents and Mr. Robinson (against Mrs. Robinson's decadent demands), Ben takes out the Robinsons' daughter Elaine during her visit down from college.

> **Maybe it's about a boy who saves himself through madness.**
>
> **—Director Mike Nichols' reply to producer Lawrence Turman's question as to what was the theme of *The Graduate***

Guilty, resentful, and conflicted, he drags the Berkeley student on a reckless ride into Hollywood where he humiliates her in a strip bar. Only when her honest tears make him face his own infantile aggression does he drop his bad-boy act and befriend this beautiful young woman. The rest of their night together has everything his postcollege life has lacked: clarity, communication, sincerity, and fun. In short, they discover they're soul mates and fall in love. The next day, Ben drives over through the rain to pick up Elaine for a day together. From the crouched car he sees a drenched and shapely pair of legs dash for the shelter of his Alfa, but it's not Elaine who jumps in but mommy dearest.

The feces hit the fan as the fanatical Mrs. R. threatens to tell her daughter all about her and Ben. Ben runs to Elaine's room to confess the deed himself. When daughter sees drenched mother staring hungrily at mumbling boyfriend, words are not necessary. So begins Ben's battle to win back the woman he was made for, though it means defying, defiling, and destroying every convention he was made from. From L.A. to Berkeley to L.A. to Berkeley to a fateful wedding in Santa Barbara, it's a helluva love story and a story of its times.

Originally, producer Turman, screenwriter Henry, and director Nichols had envisioned the Braddocks and Robinsons as the quintessential healthy, blonde, fit, and feckless Angelenos—"Surfboards," as Henry called them. The team's dream cast was Robert Redford as Ben (who turned the part down), Candace Bergen as Elaine, and Ronald Reagan and Doris Day as Ben's parents.

All that changed when Henry and Nichols saw a scrawny, ethnic, decidedly unhandsome actor named Dustin Hoffman on stage in New York in Ronald Ribman's play *Harry, Noon and Night*. Hoffman played a crippled German transvestite, and as Henry said, "It was impossible to believe that he wasn't at least one or two of those things." The trio powwowed and rationalized that Ben could be what Henry termed a "genetic throwback" from the homogenous perfection of his family.

The actor, however, was skeptical of the Hollywood interest and stubbornly refused to sign the obligatory six-picture contract before flying west to what he considered a futile audition (the contract held whoever landed Ben to six more pictures of Paramount's choosing). Meeting the casual Nichols at a swank studio bar on the lot, Hoffman felt immediately inadequate to the Hollywood glitz. Katharine Ross's performance in the thriller *Games* (1967) and the petitioning that her costar, the great Simone Signoret, did on her behalf landed Ross an interview and Hoffman's bad dream turned into "a Jewish nightmare." He couldn't imagine himself paired with such beauty. "I'd never asked a girl in acting class to do a love scene before," Hoffman admitted. "No girl asked me either." For Ross' part, she remembered, "He [Hoffman] looked about three feet tall, so dead serious, so humorless, so unkempt. I thought the screen test was going to be a disaster."

It was and it wasn't. Before the test the following day in the upholstered chair of a makeup department that looked to Hoffman "like an operating room," wizards applied their corrective cosmetics to him for two hours. Nichols came in and asked if they could pluck Hoffman's seemingly single eyebrow, shade his substantial nose, and reduce the girth of his sixteen-and-a-half-inch (42cm) neck.

The test itself was even more humiliating. Hoffman, a slow study, and Ross both consistently went up on their ten pages of lines. To relieve the mounting stress, Hoffman impulsively, playfully, misguidedly pinched Ross' behind during a take, causing her to scream at him. After an entire day of takes Hoffman packed it in. Shaking hands with each of the crew members who had been on the set, he accidentally pulled out of his pocket a handful of New York subway tokens, which spilled all over the floor. The grip picked them up, handed them to Hoffman, and said, "Here, kid. You're gonna need these."

Back in New York the dejected Hoffman had no idea that his honesty, openness, and genuine flusteredness after the fanny

*OPPOSITE: How do you tell your girl you're seeing someone else ... her mother? Dustin Hoffman is going to give it the post-college try with Katharine Ross as (above) her mother tries to bridge the generation gap in* **The Graduate (1967).**

*The Eye of the Beholder, or Get Out Your Preconceptions* **101**

pinch had made him the only choice for Ben. Instructed by his agent to call Nichols at his house, Hoffman forgot the time difference and actually woke the director up, only to hear the sacred words, "Well, you got it." The actor may have had an inkling of what elderly *Hollywood Reporter* columnist Radie Harris would point to him and say more than a year later when she recognized him at the screening he was sneaking out of: "Young man, life is never going to be the same for you."

It's hard to find anything about *The Graduate* that isn't worthy of praise. Hoffman's (Ben), Ross's (Elaine), and Anne Bancroft's (Mrs. Robinson) acting is as excellent as it is natural. As Nichols noted from Hoffman's audition, "He appeared to be simply living his life without pretending." This naturalness in the film wasn't unplanned. The cast (originally with Gene Hackman as Mr. Robinson until he was replaced by Murray Hamilton) rehearsed for three weeks using chalk marks and prop furniture. Nichols "knew the right questions," remembers Hoffman, who because of his ten-year seniority to Ben approached the lead role as "a character part."

Ben's flustered foibles in the company of his seductress came after Nichols asked Hoffman who his childhood idol was. The answer? His big brother Ronnie, who always held his breath and exhaled in spurts when he was nervous. Dustin snorted away in rehearsal. When Bancroft suggested that he drop the mannerism and let the essence remain, Ben's high-pitched squeals and toots of distress emerged.

In the hysterical scene where Ben tries to get a hotel room (under the assumed name of Gladstone) from hotel desk clerk Buck Henry ("Are you here for an affair, sir?" meaning a wedding reception), Nichols had asked his star to approach it as if he were buying condoms for the first time. The resulting nuance is priceless. Before the big hotel-room seduction scene, Nichols took Hoffman aside and asked him about the first time he ever touched a girl as an adolescent. Hoffman recalled a high school trick of walking upstairs putting on his jacket as a developed classmate was walking down and the opportunity it gave him to stretch out his hand for a first feel.

Taking that supersuaveness into the scene, Hoffman walked up behind Bancroft as she was removing her shirt and stealthily cupped his hand over the right cup of her brassiere. When the uninformed Bancroft, who was wearing falsies, didn't notice the grope, a humiliated Hoffman remained motionless for several seconds and then walked to the wall and began pounding his head against it to keep from laughing. Nichols let the camera roll.

This isn't to say that Nichols couldn't motivate by other means. When an irate Elaine bursts into Ben's rented room in San Francisco (where he has tracked her), Nichols had Ross run up three flights of stairs for every take. Eventually, she just had to sit down on Ben's bed, exhaustion tempering the anger the character was feeling. The scene is as real and achingly romantic as they come.

When the notoriously stubborn and temperamental Hoffman was exhausted in another scene, Nichols whispered in his ear, "This is the only day we're ever going to shoot this scene, and no matter how exhausted or lousy you feel, I want you to remember that what you give me is going to be on celluloid for people to see forever and ever. I know you're tired, but when you go to see this film, if you don't like your work in this scene, just remember always this was the day you screwed up." That was enough anxiety to galvanize Hoffman into excellence.

The acting isn't the only seamless thing about *The Graduate*. Every element seems to raise the film's stature. Robert Surtees' cinematography is incredibly innovative. The first frames of extreme close-ups give you an inescapable feeling of Ben's isolation, as does one surreal scene that involves underwater photography. Later a swirling, sensual sequence taking Ben in a seamless cycle from the realities of his pool and bedroom at home to Mrs. Robinson's bed is almost magical.

Henry's work on the script is no less stellar. When, on their fateful night out, Elaine drags Ben to the bar at the Taft Hotel (despite Ben's pretense of not knowing the hotel) and he is greeted by name by what seems like every member of the hotel staff, it's hard not to laugh so hard you can't hear. Later scenes of Ben's yearning for the Elaine he has alienated are heartbreaking. Henry's take on "a story of one guy's desperation to connect with one person" is at one point distilled to an overhead glimpse of Ben writing his love's name over and over again (something Henry himself had done in his youth). The deliciously ambiguous ending (on a bus) may not be saccharine but it certainly is not a cop-out.

With Simon and Garfunkel's now-classic soundtrack (including "Sounds of Silence" and "Mrs. Robinson") woven throughout, this story of coming of age, falling in love, and breaking away seems like the ultimate convergence of every element that makes a great movie. (So great that Buck Henry appears as himself in Robert Altman's *The Player*, 1992, to pitch the sequel where, according to Hoffman, a middle-aged Ben sleeps with his son's girlfriend.) Ironically, the one feature most commonly attributed to creative genius was simple necessity. Hoffman's much-ballyhooed Christlike tableau standing against the enormous window of a Santa Barbara church was not always brilliantly symbolic. Originally, the earnest actor's pounding fists threatened to shatter the huge plate of glass, which was a gift to the church. When the horror-stricken priest threatened to kick the invading film crew out, Hoffman was forced to spread his arms and pound in two different places. This is a film that's brilliant even when it's just trying to make do.

**OPPOSITE: Dustin Hoffman and Katharine Ross set matrimony back a hundred years...or is that forward...in The Graduate (1967)? RIGHT: Behind the bench and behind closed doors, even the most loving couple can get in each other's faces when one is the prosecutor (Spencer Tracy) and the other is the defense attorney (Katharine Hepburn) for a murder trial, as in the feisty and fun Adam's Rib (1950).**

# CALLING A TRUCE IN THE BATTLE OF THE SEXES

*M*aybe men really are from Mars and women really are from Venus. Maybe the battle of the sexes is a war that can't help but be waged. Maybe these opposites that attract, these yins and yangs, these chromosomal complements were never really meant to understand each other. Maybe true friendship without sexual complication is impossible between the sexes.

The eighties had already tackled a dazzling list of love issues in big Hollywood films. Movies embraced a May-September romance in *Atlantic City* (1980) and observed obsession and social stigma in *The French Lieutenant's Woman* (1981). They cross-dressed up to see how the other half lives and loves in *Tootsie* (1982) and *Victor/Victoria* (1982). They helped us come to terms with the death of a loved one in *Terms of Endearment* (1983) and infidelity in *Falling in Love* (1984). Man learned to love his fellow man and woman learned to love and lose herself in her fellow woman in *Kiss of the Spider Woman* (1985) and *Desperately Seeking Susan* (1985). Audiences even got insight into the Lord's romantic inclinations in

the controversial *The Last Temptation of Christ* (1988). Still, where was the movie to address the basic conundrum of heterogeneous friendship?

Rob Reiner had perused, updated, and rejuvenated Frank Capra's mismatched romance *It Happened One Night* (1934) with a cross-country journey to discovery for college classmates John Cusack and Daphne Zuniga in *The Sure Thing* (1985). Reiner had examined formative male friendship in *Stand by Me* (1986). On the singles social-relations question he was not about to glibly say, "Why ask why?" He was going to find out.

After his divorce from director/actress Penny Marshall, Reiner himself was back in the dating world and not exactly loving it. "I had women friends and sex always seemed to surface in one way or another," he remembered. "I just wondered if men and women really could be friends without sex coming into it." While working on *The Princess Bride* (1987), Reiner discussed this as a theme for a movie with producer Andrew Scheinman and romantic-comedy writer Nora Ephron (who would bring Reiner into the picture for her directorial debut, *Sleepless in Seattle*, 1993). To get the male perspective, Ephron (whose own divorce from journalist Carl

Bernstein had yielded plenty of sexually barbed humor in her novel and screenplay for *Heartburn*, 1986) interviewed Reiner and Scheinman for three solid days about their romantic pasts and learned perhaps more than she ever wanted about the male perspective.

Out of this megahuddle, Ephron and Reiner drafted the now-famous screen story of two University of Chicago grads, Harry Burns and Sally Albright. College is over and Sally gives her best friend's boyfriend, Harry, a ride home to New York. Of course, within minutes Harry hits on her. She's totally flabbergasted. And so begins a charged and challenging sexually political butting of heads that will hilariously and heartbreakingly span the next couple of decades. Grungy, tactless, sardonic Harry is cynically convinced that a relationship between members of the opposite sex is impossible to make pure. Pert and perpetually optimistic Sally knows otherwise. With all their idiosyncrasies and beliefs, they are about as compatible as a warm beer and a cold milk shake, yet each takes a certain pleasure in each other's dogged differences.

Their ride ends in Washington Square with halfhearted offers from Harry to get together with the newcomer to the Big Apple. But nothing happens… until they meet on a plane five years later. He's a political consultant who's about to get married. She's a writer for *People* magazine who's madly in love. Neither have changed their basic thinking, but they now have the maturity and happiness to accept each other's differences without getting on each other's nerves. While a friendship might be fruitful, their lives sweep them apart once again.

Five years later things are very different. His marriage is kaput. Her romance went belly-up. They've both been doing some hard thinking. In their mutual wounded bafflement with the other sex they form a friendship and, as Reiner says, "are ready to go about the business of really rubbing up against each other." They rub with their minds, supporting and challenging each other. Harry and Sally even take a stab at matchmaking for each other with their respective best friends, Jess and Marie (Bruno Kirby and Carrie Fisher). The two friends fall for each other instead. Harry and Sally are left to be each other's best friend. But the question is, are they meant to be more?

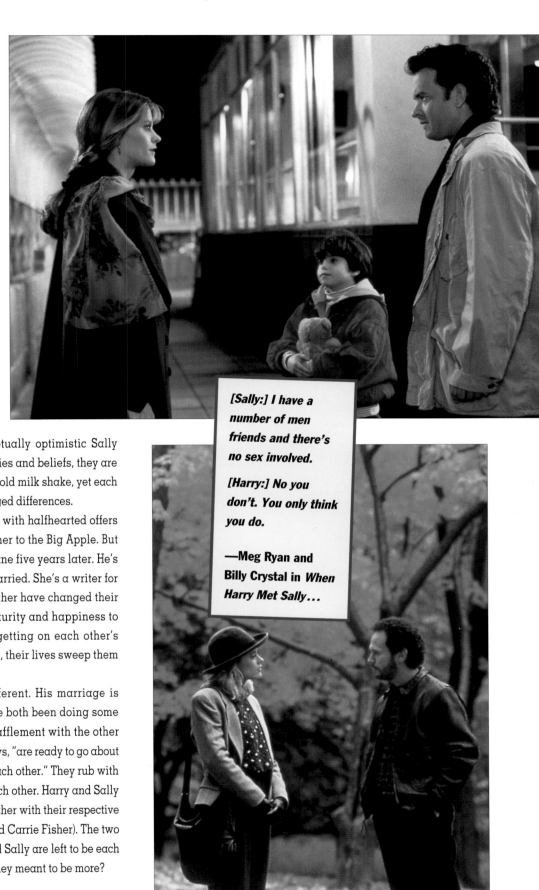

[Sally:] I have a number of men friends and there's no sex involved.

[Harry:] No you don't. You only think you do.

—Meg Ryan and Billy Crystal in *When Harry Met Sally…*

*OPPOSITE: Dustin Hoffman (right if you didn't guess) is just trying to discover the woman within, but will Jessica Lange understand in* Tootsie *(1982)? ABOVE: Meg Ryan is hoping she's found Mister Right (and son) in Tom Hanks, but could she be wrong in* Sleepless in Seattle *(1993)? RIGHT: Friendship, love, animosity, and orgasms in restaurants—it's all there* When Harry Met Sally *(1989).*

We begin to think so. After decades of borough-bashing movies, Harry and Sally make their way through a New York even more romantic than Woody Allen's *Manhattan* (1979): museums, autumn leaves, the Central Park boathouse, brownstones and bistros, New Year's Eve parties at the glamorous Puck Building, crisp days at Giants Stadium, and Harry's spacious apartment that commands either the most romantic or lonely view (the Empire State Building) in the world. As production designer Jane Musky would later say, "Rob and I felt that we could keep throwing the two of them into the most romantic situations possible, which would be so obvious to everyone else, if not to them." What's in the stars for these two scarred lonely hearts? If sex ever enters the picture, will their friendship survive?

To cast this conundrum of a film ("Harry is an extension of me to some degree"), Reiner eventually called on the services of his old friend Billy Crystal. A couple of decades earlier, Norman Lear had written Crystal into an episode of *All in the Family* as Mike Stivic's (Reiner) best buddy. Off the set, Billy and Rob compared comedic notes on everything, including headaches (for Reiner they were like rubber bands being tightened across his eyes; for Crystal it was like Buddy Rich tuning up at the back of his neck). Soon they were on the phone comparing notes on movies they were watching

on TV (just like Harry and Sally do with *Casablanca*, 1942). Over the years, the boys hung out so much together that, in Crystal's words, "If we lived next door to each other, we'd be connected with two paper cups and a string."

Reiner, however, had never seen his friend in a role as complex as Harry, and despite the fact that Ephron "went through almost the entire casting process praying that Rob would come to his senses and play the part," he first went after bigger fish. But Richard Dreyfuss wanted more scenes showing Harry away from Sally, and Tom Hanks and Albert Brooks also passed.

Meanwhile, Crystal confessed, "In the back of my mind I had been wondering, 'Why isn't he talking to me about this thing?' Inside I was dying a little bit. Then one night he called. It was almost like he had been cheating on his wife or something. He said, 'I had to see everybody, I had to go through the process just to make

**ABOVE: Always the bridesmaid, never the bride. Sally (Meg Ryan) looks less than thrilled for friends Jess (Bruno Kirby) and Marie (Carrie Fisher), but Harry (Billy Crystal) doesn't seem to get it.... OPPOSITE:... Then again, sometimes it takes a guy a while for things to sink in.**

sure you're the perfect guy'." When Crystal demurred, "I haven't read it yet. What if I don't like it?" Reiner countered, "I guarantee you'll like it. You'll hear your voice in it." Crystal did, and for the first time said yes without even consulting his agent or manager. "I could see myself having a field day with this guy," he said.

The comedian's invention was invaluable in providing finishing touches to the script. The bizarre voice that Harry teaches Sally in the "Temple of Dendur sequence" came from a bartender Crystal knew. He successfully lobbied for a scene where Harry and Sally bump into Harry's ex-wife. His heartfelt confession of pain over the breakup of his marriage to his pal Jess was punctuated by their participation in "the wave" while sitting in the stands during a football game ("Rob and I have always talked about the most depressing stuff while we're doing something else"). And perhaps his most memorable contribution was hitting it off in the car with Sally by spitting a grape seed out of what he mistakes for an open window. Splat!

Reiner selected stellar comedienne Meg Ryan to complete the other half of the yin-yang circle. Ephron termed her "a writer's dream of an actress because she will get a laugh wherever you know there is a laugh. And she will get a laugh wherever you hope there is a laugh. And she will get a laugh where in your wildest dreams you never thought it was possible to squeeze one out." Ryan does, viewing the script as if "someone had been eavesdropping on my conversations for the past ten years" and crediting Crystal and Reiner for making her feel welcome into the closeness of their "pre-fab relationship."

Crystal's Harry sees "women as sort of a service station. You pull in every so often, get gas and oil and then you just go on your way." In one scene (that will come back to haunt him), he confides to Sally that immediately after a single man has finished making love with a woman at her place, he is wondering how long he has to hold her in his arms before he can get up and go home ("Is thirty seconds enough?"). Reiner wanted something for Sally to divulge where Harry along with the men in the audience would have their turn saying, "Is that true?" while the women in the audience said, "Yes, we've all done that." Ephron suggested Sally fill Harry in on the fact that women sometimes fake orgasm. Ryan said "I can do fake orgasm." Reiner said, "Why don't we put it in some incongruous place like a deli?"

In what critic Charles Champlin called a scene "that would have given Will Hays, Joe Breen and the whole Production Code staff collective apoplexy," Sally proves over lunch that the dismissive Harry ("I've never had any complaints") wouldn't necessarily notice the unreal thing if he were on top of it.

On the day of the shoot, when Ryan was understandably reticent about climaxing in front of a sea of crew, extras, and countermen in Katz's Delicatessen, Reiner told her, "Meg, it's in a deli. It's not a sex thing. It's comedy." With that in mind, she was soon pounding the table in one of the funniest (and sexiest) sequences in film history. It was so incredible that the deli staff awarded her a jumbo salami tied with a big, red bow. And to top it all off, Reiner gave his own mother, Estelle (who had told him the story of a family friend who had faked orgasm for her husband-to-be and was upset because "she made him think that was that way it was. Then she had to do it every time"), the punch line to end all punch lines.

Crystal faced challenges of his own. "When you're playing a funny scene, Rob and that big, great cute head of his is behind the camera rooting and laughing—and a lot of times he'd laugh during the take!" he bemoaned. "You'd hear this 'ha ha ha' and they'd yell 'cut!' I'd say 'Rob would you please get off the set, do something—get a muzzle!'" Joking aside, Crystal took the matter of taking on Harry's very unfunny pain very seriously. "I didn't live at the same hotel as Rob. I chose to live alone. I got every sad Frank Sinatra record I could. I didn't call home as much. And when I'd call people, I'd call Meg or spend a lot of time with Bruno."

The very genuine balance between humor and heartbreak is met in *When Harry Met Sally*…. The friendship issue, the romance issue, the differences issue, the traps, the triumphs, and the truths of modern romance are all explored by Reiner et al. with love, laughs, and lucidity. As to whether men and women can ever just be friends without sex coming into it, Reiner assures, "You can… for a while."

# PLAYING THE RACE CARD

*W*hite girls may have sung the praises of "black boys" and black girls crooned just as euphorically about "white boys" in the sixties Broadway musical *Hair* (with black and white army officers campily singing it in Milos Forman's 1979 movie adaptation). *Guess Who's Coming to Dinner* (1967) and a spate of "conscious" movies from the same period might have opened the door even further on celebrating interracial romance. Still, a vast majority of similar cinematic stories involving people of different skin tones don't exactly end on an up note. There are movies like the recent, excellent rendering of *Othello* (1996) (with an actual black man, Laurence Fishburne, playing Othello no less), where true love ends in disaster. And there are many more where passion is drowned out in polemics and love story gets lost in the sociopolitical shuffle. It's a breath of fresh air when a movie manages to be about race and romance in equal parts and where the racism is more complex than the usual slobbering stereotype.

Indian-born, Harvard-educated, thirty-five-year-old former documentarian Mira Nair was on what independent filmmakers call the "rape and pillage" tour—in other words, promoting the hell out of her Oscar-nominated, Cannes Camera d'Or and Prix du Publique award–winning film of Indian street kids, *Salaam Bombay!* (1988). While in Tinseltown, she was invited by many a mogul to pitch her next story idea. Inspired by an article by Jane Kramer in *The New Yorker* concerning an Indian Muslim family that had expatriated to London (where they were too dark) when General Idi Amin had expelled all "Asians" from Uganda in 1972 (because they were too light), she had something special to pitch.

"I had been drawn to the idea of making a film that dealt in some way with the hierarchy of color, a film about an interracial love story," stated Nair, though she was well aware of how such films usually fared at the box office. Yet racial identity fascinated her, and even in India color was an issue. "Fair is equated with beauty and dark with what is not beautiful," she admitted, and skin creams were sold to make dark skin fairer.

Nair envisioned a meeting between a "proud African-American man who has never lived in Africa" and a "spirited Indian woman who has never lived in India," all on the soil of the good ol' U.S.A. This epic made "on a peanut" would be financed with money from several different continents and shot in two countries. It would internationally groove to Muslim love songs, African pop renditions of music from Indian films, Delta blues, and gospel. And it would feature seventy-nine speaking roles including a Hollywood star, a complete unknown, and actors from all over the map. If you like a delicious mix, *Mississippi Masala* (1992) (Masala is a spicy mix of flavors in Indian cooking) makes for one of the best sleepers you'll ever see.

Indians had originally been brought to Africa to build the East African Railway in the late 1800s. When Amin demanded "Africa for Africans," 75 percent of the Indians' descendants, born and bred in Uganda, Kenya, and Tanzania, found themselves fleeing their

**ABOVE: Sidney Poitier and Katherine Houghton broke new ground as lovebirds who just didn't happen to be of the same feather in Guess Who's Coming to Dinner (1967).**
**OPPOSITE: Spice it up! That's what carpet-cleaning Denzel Washington and motel-working daughter of India Sarita Choudhury do in Mira Nair's tangy but tender Mississippi Masala (1992).**

PASSION. TRADITION.
MIX IT UP.

—Publicity line for
Mira Nair's
*Mississippi Masala*
(1992)

homeland. Nair wanted to follow one family on its terrifying exodus all the way to Greenwood, Mississippi, a locale where Indians had such a lock on the motel business that "you often have to look very hard to find an American-run motel."

There, years later, in a minor traffic accident in a borrowed car, the family's beautiful twenty-four-year-old daughter, Mina (who works as a maid and clerk in a family-run motel), literally runs into a handsome, small-time carpet-cleaning entrepreneur, Demetrius. When her family freaks out at the prospect of falling victim to the great American pastime—lawsuits—it's up to Mina to make peace. She makes more than peace.

Before the Oscars, Nair spent a month living in Indian motels all over Mississippi. After the Oscars, she returned with her old Harvard roommate, scriptwriter Sooni Traporevala, for a few more weeks in the small town of Greenwood, where they met many Indians "haunted" by wistful memories of Uganda. Then it was off to Kenya and Uganda "to look firsthand at what the Indians had left." By August they had a script to show Denzel Washington, who had backed out of the interracial romance *Love Field* (1992) but who loved *Mississippi Masala*. "Denzel was instrumental in guiding us towards finding out more about the black world in this story," admitted Nair. It was back to Greenwood for a couple of weeks.

Back in Hollywood, script and star in hand, Nair found most possible distributors uncomfortable with the largely nonwhite cast. One producer even asked, "Can't you find room for a white protagonist?" to which Nair responded, "All the waiters in this film will be white." Luckily, the Samuel Goldwyn Company came through. The director saw seventy-five women in L.A., New York, and Chicago in her quest for the right Mina. None of them projected the right combination of "intelligence with feistiness and sensuality" to make Mina "unselfconsciously attractive." Off to London for casting consultant Suzy Figgis' help in rounding up twenty-five more candidates from local actresses, models, and students.

Only one photo caught Nair's eye. "It was torn and completely disheveled, and a bit out of focus," she remembered, "but the woman in the photo had this mass of hair and this beautiful mouth and she didn't look the least bit interested in being photographed. It was so different from the droves of slick glossies of smiling creatures begging you to hire them that I'd seen." The malcontent was film student Sarita Choudhury, who when she showed up to meet Nair was so unkempt that Figgis immediately sent her to a salon to get spiffed up. Choudhury was of Indian ancestry but born in Jamaica (look for her Bob Marley T-shirt in an early scene) and wanted to meet Nair with hopes of becoming a production intern. As she said, "Things didn't quite work out that way."

Nair assembled her eclectic cast in Mississippi for ten days of rehearsal. Charles S. Dutton, who starred on Broadway in August Wilson's *The Piano Lesson*, would play Demetrius' flirtatious brother, Tyrone, who hits on Mina by asking her, "Hey, are you Mexican?" (Barroom locals who had used such lines on Mira and Sooni were brought in to give Tyrone's dialogue their stamp of approval.) Mina's wounded father, Jay, would be played by the celebrated veteran of such films as *Ghandi* (1982) and *My Beautiful Laundrette* (1985), Roshan Seth. Mina's mom, Kinnu, went to Indian actress Sharmila Tagore (who looks uncannily like Choudhury), who had started at the age of fifteen in the films of the great Indian director, Satyjit Ray, and who went on to fame in Hindu musical films.

Local whites, worried about another film depicting southern bigotry, were mollified with the glamorous-looking Nair's word that she was just shooting "a love story." Indeed it was. There is such a natural tenderness and spark between these two tremendously likable working people that you are rooting for them as soon as you meet them. Choudhury's unactorlike and uncanny combination of unaffected spunk and love-goddess looks is impossible to resist. Washington's genuineness and quiet workingman's cool (with lines like "Do you mind if I kiss you?") are devastating. Their love scene together positively smolders. "We didn't look at it sexually," Choudhury insists. "We approached it like a slow dance. For us it was a very quiet, slow, evolving thing." Nevertheless, its heat has fiery consequences.

A day-to-day feeling of family, with its prizes and pitfalls, pervades every scene on each side of this film's color line. From backyard barbecues to wedding receptions to line dancing at the local bar, both Demetrius and Mina are plunged into each other's variation of American culture. Unfortunately, as Demetrius says, "Racism is passed down like family recipes." Even though he bravely maintains that "the trick is you got to know what to eat and what to leave on your plate," the loving couple's plight with their families, their community, and ultimately each other is riveting.

This marvelous movie doesn't stop there, but goes on to beautiful Uganda (where Nair invited Choudhury along for the ride for the first film shot there since *The African Queen*, 1951) for a final screen resolution to the film's other love (love of country) that is as powerful as it is wordlessly eloquent. *Mississippi Masala*, like the more recent *A Family Thing* (1996), pulls as few punches as it pushes buttons. In short, it's a film for our future. "Even though the film is irreverent and sometimes wicked," maintains Nair, "it's a film which genuinely loves its characters which is how I see life. I could hope that people seeing this film will be able to see themselves in it, that this is not just a film about The Other." See for your "Self."

*Jackie Kennedy–obsessed hairdresser Michelle Pfeiffer makes friends with the uneasy Dennis Haysbert and his daughter Stephanie McFadden on a bus ride through troubled times in* **Love Field** *(1991).*

# There's a Plot for Us... Somewhere a Plot for Us

*See if you can match up the movie with the thumbnail description of the color-blind couple in question.*

## COUPLE

1. She's married to a missionary. He's a Chinese warlord.

2. She's blind as a bat. He's her boyfriend.

3. She's hiding out in drag in the Old West. He's a runaway from the railroad.

4. He's an architect. She's his new secretary.

5. She's a working mom. He's a sperm-bank donor.

6. She's a widowed teacher. He's beautiful, bald, etc., etc....

7. She's a refuge. He's her homicidal sergeant husband.

8. She's a Canadian orphan. He's the Eskimo who learns to fly.

9. He's a Japanese gentleman. She's a Jewish mother.

10. She's an actress. He's an airman.

11. She's a shark. He's a jet.

12. He's a tender terrorist. She's a "surprising" chanteuse.

13. He's a captive. She'll be his wife.

14. He's a pizza-delivery guy. She needs an ice cube to cool down.

15. He's an explorer. She's a pubescent princess.

16. She's a pregnant teen. He's a sailor on leave.

17. She's an old, German floor washer. He's an inarticulate mechanic.

18. She's a hooker. He's her chauffeur.

19. He's a Pennsylvania coal miner. She's one of the last women on earth.

20. He's an artist. She's a model hooker.

## MOVIE

A: Annabella Sciorra and Wesley Snipes in Jungle Fever *(1991)*

B: Rita Tushingham and Murray Melvin in A Taste of Honey *(1961)*

C: Suzy Amis and David Chung in The Legend of Little Joe *(1993)*

D: Spike Lee and Rosie Perez in Do the Right Thing *(1989)*

E: Whoopi Goldberg and Ted Danson in Made in America *(1993)*

F: Miyoshi Umeki and Marlon Brando in Sayonara *(1957)*

G: Barbara Stanwyck and Toshia Mori in The Bitter Tea of General Yen *(1933)*

H: Deborah Kerr and Yul Brynner in The King and I *(1956)*

I: Anne Parillaud and Jason Scott Lee in Map of the Human Heart *(1993)*

J: Cathy Tyson and Bob Hoskins in Mona Lisa *(1986)*

K: Harry Belafonte and Inger Stevens in The World, the Flesh, and the Devil *(1959)*

L: Hiep Thi Le and Tommy Lee Jones in Heaven and Earth *(1993)*

M: Brigitte Mira and El Hedi Ben Salem in Ali—Fear Eats the Soul *(1974)*

N: Corinna Tsopei and Richard Harris in A Man Called Horse *(1970)*

O: Alec Guinness and Rosalind Russell in A Majority of One *(1962)*

P: Stephen Rea and Jaye Davidson in The Crying Game *(1992)*

Q: Mel Gibson and Irene Bedard in Pocahontas *(1994)*

R: William Holden and Nancy Kwan in The World of Suzie Wong *(1960)*

S: Elizabeth Hartman and Sidney Poitier in A Patch of Blue *(1965)*

T: Natalie Wood and Richard Beymer in West Side Story *(1961)*

**Answers**

1=G, 2=S, 3=C, 4=A, 5=E, 6=H, 7=L, 8=I, 9=O, 10=F, 11=T, 12=P, 13=N, 14=D, 15=Q, 16=B, 17=M, 18=J, 19=K, 20=R

# A Woman's Place Is in the Kitchen... the Bedroom... the World!

*D*on't read or watch the following if you are either hungry or sexually repressed. The multicourse feral feast for two in *Tom Jones* (1963) may have set your heart afire and your stomach growling. Figs may have gotten you hot under the Victorian collar in *Women in Love* (1969). The egg slurping in *Tampopo* (1986) may have left you hard-boiled. The erotic eatery in *Eat Drink Man Woman* (1994) may have made you sizzle to be sated. But watch Like *Water for Chocolate* (1992) and you just might spontaneously ignite.

Many a fantastical love story has taught us many a delicious lesson in life. Antoine Artaud's surreal *Beauty and the Beast* (1946) taught us about the humanizing power of true love (and dig those Daliesque human-arm candelabras). *Splash* (1984) and its mermaid heroine, like the hero of *Edward Scissorhands* (1990), helped us embrace the bizzare in those we love. The truly amazing *Truly Madly Deeply* (1991) showed us a ghost's commitment to come back and help his lonesome loved one get on with life. Alfonso Arau's magical, mythical, feminist film based on the best-selling novel *Like Water for Chocolate*, written by his wife, Laura Esquivel, shows us that it's never too late to set your heart free, learn from the

> *Acted with subtle ferocity, directed with expansive tenderness,* **Like Water for Chocolate** *[1992] is a story of passion in bondage and death in a firestorm of desire too long withheld. Viewers need not feel so constrained; they can enjoy the emotional splendor, gasp at the ghosts, cry with as much good cause as Tita. By comparison with this banquet of feelings, most other movies are trail mix.*
>
> **—Richard Corlis,**
> *Time* **magazine, April 5, 1993**

mistakes of others, or immerse yourself in that divine cauldron of ritual and pleasure called the kitchen.

But why the strange title? As its author states, "In Mexico, hot chocolate is made with water, not milk. To prepare the drink, one brings the water to a boil and then adds the cocoa. When someone becomes extremely agitated it is said that they are 'like water for chocolate.' This expression is also used to describe a state of sexual arousal." By the time of the film, the book (originally published "in twelve monthly installments with recipes, romances and home remedies") had already seen nine printings in Mexico and translations into eleven languages in more than twenty countries.

Set on a Rio Grande rancho in the desert region that joins Mexico with its neighbor to the north, it tells the story of Tita through a cookbook/diary passed down to her niece. Things are strange from the start. In the womb, Tita starts crying because of the onions being cut in the kitchen by her mother, Dona Elena, and Nacha, the family cook. Tears flow so much that when her mother's water breaks, there is such a flood that the salt is dried and stored in a forty-pound (18kg) sack.

By 1910, when Tita is a young woman, life is no banquet. Her father has died of shock upon being informed that his wife bore Tita's sister, Gertrudis, with a mulatto. Since then Dona has hardened and claimed a tradition where Tita, the youngest, will never marry and must take care of her until she dies. As a consequence, under Nacha's tutelage, Tita has become a sorceress in the kitchen.

This wizardry and her unaffected beauty has bewitched a neighboring landowner's handsome son, Pedro, who professes love to Tita (appropriately enough while she is up the larder ladder just after she has scalded dough in boiling oil) and asks for her hand in marriage. Dona cruelly rejects the offer. Pedro, unable to buck tradition and kidnap his love, settles for marrying Tita's sister, Rosaura, to be as near Tita as possible. The trouble begins. When Tita makes the cake for her sister's wedding to her own boyfriend (Dona has made her prepare the whole banquet), her tears drop into the mix.

Her emotions are so strong and true that every wedding guest who takes a delicious bite becomes suffused with her sadness, remembering their own personal grief. They cry so much that they vomit into the nearby river. Nacha cries so much that she dies, and since Rosaura can't cook a thing, Tita has a new job. When Pedro brings her a love token of roses (and Dona demands they be thrown away), Tita innocently decides to use the petals in cooking quail. However, the thorns prick her and a drop of her hot blood gets into the following sauce:

---

CHABELA WEDDING CAKE

INGREDIENTS

175 grams refined granulated sugar

300 grams cake flour (sifted three times)

17 eggs

1 peel of lime, grated

Multiply by ten.

---

QUAIL IN ROSE-PETAL SAUCE

INGREDIENTS

12 roses, preferably red

12 chestnuts

2 teaspoons of butter

2 drops attar of roses

2 tablespoons honey

2 cloves of garlic

6 quail

---

**OPPOSITE: Lumi Cavazos plays a daughter seemingly destined to cook instead of love in the marvelous, mythical Mexican Like Water for Chocolate (1993). ABOVE: Yet even she gets out of the kitchen sometimes (here with Marco Leonardi) with fiery results.**

You can imagine the results. Each diner is aroused beyond reckoning. The beautiful Gertrudis actually starts to smolder; running to the bathhouse to shower away her heat, she sets it on fire. Fleeing the flames naked into the desert, she is snatched up by a revolutionary riding by and they manage to make love on horseback before disappearing into the sunset. That night the inflamed Pedro can no longer put off making love to his wife, Rosaura.

Let it suffice to say that Tita's story is a long and engrossing one with as many twists as there are recipes. Pedro and Tita's destiny spans generations, involves resurrections, insurrections, extremes of cruelty (Dona) and kindness (an Anglo doctor named John Brown), battles with ghosts and insanity, a shawl as long as Mexico, the worst case of flatulence in recorded history, and a magical ending that will literally burn itself into your memory.

Expert cook Esquivel wrote the book in homage to her great-great-aunt, who was denied marriage three times and cared for her mother until the age of ninety-two. She believed that the kitchen turns the traditional sexual power structure topsy-turvy. After all, she says, it's where "women penetrate men's bodies through their food in which they have put their very essence." Sound magical? Lo Real Maravilloso (Magic Realism), a term coined by Cuban writer Alejo Carpentier, abounds here as in much of Latin literature. "It shows that we live in different dimensions at the same time," says the sixty-two-year-old director. Although at first Arau didn't want to direct his wife's (of eighteen years) screenplay because he "felt very insecure about the feminine perspective," he acceded when she kept rejecting the women directors he rounded up.

As Arau proceeded with the project, he came to believe that one of the film's purposes was to show that "now that women have achieved certain successes, perhaps it is time to take a look at what has been lost in the process: some of their superpowers." He gives an example: "In Mexico there's a belief when you are making tamales. If the people who are making them are in a bad mood, the tamales will never cook. So you have to bring other people to talk to the tamales with good will to get them to cook. This is totally real for us," he insists. "So what I did was make the magical things matter of fact."

There is mucho magic in the film thanks to husband and wife's shared vision and a flawless but surprising cast. As Tita, Lumi Cavazos is the underdog with the face of an angel. Each emotion seems to surface on her with painful and beautiful clarity. As the mama from hell, Regina Torne turns Dona Elena into one of the most despicable screen villainesses to ever frost a frame. Eighty-year-old Luis Buñuel film veteran Ada Carrasco is a cook/nanny any kid would cherish. Mario Ivan Martinez is superb as the open-hearted Anglo doctor who falls in love with Tita. Yareli Arizmendi (Rosaura) is as divinely drippy as Claudette Maille (Gertrudis) is fiery. However, Pedro wasn't Mexican at all—not even Spanish. You might remember Mario Leonardi as the adolescent star of Italian cinema's hit Cinema Paradiso (1988). The young actor wanted the role so much that he phonetically memorized the Spanish lines (which were ultimately dubbed over because of his heavy Italian accent).

Any special effects "come from the desert itself," says Arau. "When I saw the light in the Coahuila desert, I was convinced that this film could be made nowhere else." After winning eighteen major international awards, becoming Mexico's celebrated contender for the 1992 Oscar for Best Foreign Film, and nudging past I Am Curious Yellow (1969) to become the biggest-grossing foreign film of all time, it seems this wife-and-husband collaboration from the kitchen couldn't have been made by anyone else, either.

Maybe magic was in the air during the making of Like Water for Chocolate. Or maybe it was just because the shoot lasted seventeen weeks and was twenty miles from the nearest town. Twenty-two-year-old Lumi (Tita) and twenty-five-year-old Mario (Pedro) really did fall in love. "One day we were friends, and the next we were in love," admitted the bewildered Leonardi. Cavazos added that "the chemistry between us made our love scenes much better."

After visiting his parents in Rome and hers in Mexico, they moved to an even more magical place—Hollywood—where they share an apartment and a pit bull named Ben-Hur, and (hate to burst your bubble) Mario does most of the cooking. While his specialty is spaghetti carbonara, he might use the following mole recipe for turkey from the book. You'll have to watch the movie to see just what kind of effect it has. Eat hearty. Cook often. Live long. Love.

## TURKEY MOLE WITH ALMONDS AND SESAME SEEDS

### INGREDIENTS
¼ chile mulato
3 chiles pasills
3 chiles ancho
handful of almonds
handful of sesame seeds
turkey stock
1 hard roll (⅓ concha loaf)
peanuts
½ onion
wine
two tablets of chocolate
anise
lard
cloves
cinnamon
pepper
sugar
seeds from the chilis
5 cloves of garlic

# Weathering the Storm

Homosexuality as a sexual-political statement of power and beauty? We've seen it. The "love that dares not speak its name" has done so eloquently and with increasing frequency and stature in films in the past few years. Gone with the twisted. Gone with the tortured. Thanks to pioneering directors like Germany's gritty and turbulent Rainer Werner Fassbinder and Spain's excessive and erotic Pedro Almodovar, the gay perspective in cinema (as opposed to the straight perspective of homosexuality) has come out of the closet and into the screening room.

Homophobic horrors like *Cruising* (1980) aside, gay and straight directors, writers, and casts have taken gay romance out of the trembling hands of fruity hairdressers, pathetic victims, and repressed macho men and put it in the hands of nearly everybody. *My Beautiful Laundrette* made homosexuality part of the everyday for working-class English blokes. *Personal Best* (1982) gave younger lesbians license to love (and compete in the Olympics) while *Leanna* (1983) let older ones live in peace, and *Desert Hearts* (1985) dared direct a heroine to newfound happiness on that path. *Longtime Companion* (1990) offered the straight world insight to what it means to lose your lover to AIDS. The *Lost Language of Cranes* (1992) allowed a younger generation to inspire its parents to sexual honesty. *Kiss of the Spider Woman* and *Philadelphia* (1993) gave us gay heroes, and gave William Hurt and Tom Hanks Oscars to take home. *The Sum of Us* (1994) celebrated family acceptance and support of each other's lifestyle choices. Even fluff like

*Not your everyday mom and dad... just twice as loving. Nathan Lane and Robin Williams may have trod on political toes, but they did so with a light heart and a deft touch in* **The Birdcage** *(1995).*

even mated Anthony Edwards and Mare Winningham just in time for nuclear Armageddon. Dire circumstances can sharpen a lover's appreciation for the magic of the moment.

In 1993, from one of the most artistically repressive regimes in the world, came a daring love story that unflinchingly portrayed homosexuality, heterosexuality, art, and friendship through fifty years of Chinese political turmoil. Chen Kaige's *Farewell, My Concubine* (1993) is nothing less than an emotional epic, and its love triangle of protagonists include two male stars from the Peking Opera and a beautiful, strong-willed prostitute. This tangled trio will take us on a journey from the deepest pits of decadence and despair to the very pinnacles of personal sacrifice and courage. Sexual identity, the place of art in society, patriotism, and personal responsibility are just a few of the heavy topics tackled here.

In 1925, when war lords still ruled Peiping (Peking before it was a national capital), an impoverished prostitute gives her frail and quiet young son, Douzi, up to the All Luck and Happiness Academy to be fed, housed, and prepared in the brutal rigors of the opera. When refused because of his sixth finger on one of his hands, she chops it off and reapplies him.

In the grueling life of the academy, the strangely detached and beautiful Douzi is the object of ridicule for all except a charismatic troublemaker named Shitou. Together they form a bond that shelters them from the turmoil around them and vaunts each to excellence in the parts for which they are training (Douzi for the Dan role of the falsetto-singing female and Shitou for the expansive, Sheng leading-male role).

For Shitou (later known as Duan Xilou) the opera is a way to gain fame and fortune through his electric presence and command of every subtle nuance of performance. Though a loving companion to Douzi, he falls in love with and marries Juxian, the hottest hooker at the House of Blossoms. For Douzi (later known as Cheng Deyei) things are a little different. As Kaige notes, "In his world, the distinction between reality and dream, art and the state, male and female, life and death, the real and the imagined is blurred." Deyei lives for his art (looking more like a woman onstage than many women) and loves Xilou as fiercely as the concubine he

> I give them [Chinese censors] another explanation: I tell them this is not a film about homosexuality, this is a film about an artist who is in love with his art, and loves his brother artist. Sometimes you play a little game with them. You don't tell them what you think because they don't understand.
>
> —Chen Kaige on *Farewell, My Concubine* (1993)

*The Adventures of Priscilla, Queen of the Desert* (1994) and *The Birdcage* (1996) (and its predecessor, *La Cage aux Folles*, 1978) made formerly taboo sexual preference into wholesome family entertainment.

Some of the greatest love stories have long been successfully set against a backdrop of political upheaval, from Rhett and Scarlett's saga *Gone With the Wind* to Bogie and Bergman's tryst in *Casablanca*. *Yanks* (1979) brought allies like Richard Gere and Lisa Eichhorn and William Devane and Vanessa Redgrave together for the Blitz in London during World War II. *The Year of Living Dangerously* (1983) brought Mel Gibson and Sigourney Weaver together just in time for revolution in Indonesia. *Dances with Wolves* (1990) wed Kevin Costner and Mary McDonnell during the bloodshed of America's genocide against Native Americans. *Miracle Mile* (1989)

plays in the opera entitled *Farewell, My Concubine*, who kills herself to stay with her soon-to-die king. That level of passion seemingly reserved for art will engulf them all as their delicate balance is tipped by Japanese occupation, Nationalist victory, and the Cultural Revolution through Deng Xiaoping.

A young boy hangs himself for his artistic inadequacies. Another is so stirred by opera's beauty that he soils his clothes as he sits on the shoulders of a friend to watch a performance. A prostitute leaps off a thug-filled balcony into the arms of her beloved. A pregnant mother is kicked in the abdomen while trying to make peace in a rioting crowd. Betrayal comes from a child rescued from certain death on the street. A distraught star falls into the clutches of an

**OPPOSITE: Working class street punk Johnny (Daniel Day Lewis) and his middle class Indian man Omar (Gordon Warnecke) tried to find true happiness (without the starch) in My Beautiful Laundrette (1985). BELOW: Things don't work out quite as happily-ever-after for Peking Opera stars Deyei (Leslie Cheung) and Xilou (Zhang Fengyi) whose love and friendship must withstand political upheaval to boot in Chen Kaige's haunting Farewell, My Concubine (1993).**

eerie aristocrat and opium addiction. A couple burn all their possessions and make love frantically as they await invaders. A sacred sword finds a final, deadly purpose. This is not the heightened stuff of opera but the real lives of some incredibly credible characters.

Kaige found a superb cast to ride his roller coaster. As Xilou, mainland actor Zhang Fengyi, star of twenty films, is the perfect blend of rake and rational man. His cross-dressing counterpart, Deyei, is hypnotically and truly androgynously played by Hong Kong recording artist and movie celebrity Leslie Cheung. Though Kaige originally cast American star of *M. Butterfly* (1993) John Lone, he found the star's demand for a personal bodyguard, chauffeur, dresser, makeup artist, and trailer at odds with a country where the average income is the equivalent of $325 a year. Cheung, the star of such hits as John Woo's western *A Better Tomorrow* (1986), gives *The Crying Game*'s Jaye Davidson a run for his (her?) money and painstakingly learned Mandarin for the demanding role. As the tough yet tender Juxian, Gong Li, star of such triumphs as Kaige's old Beijing Film Academy classmate Zhang Yimou's tragic love story *Ju Dou* (1989) and the majestic *Raise the Red Lantern* (1991), is as flawless as her looks. Filming often became imperiled as hordes of

Chinese fans of who the press dubbed the "most beautiful woman in the world" mobbed the star, who, though escorted by fifty policemen, found her guardians too busy gawking at her to give her much protection. The mere rolling up of her stocking on the set delayed filming (and inspired Cheung to match her by rolling up his pants legs).

Far from sexy or comic is perhaps the film's most powerful scene where, under threat of hanging from the Red Guard, Xilou and Deyei both viciously renounce each other and the loyal Juxian during the confessional humiliation and finger pointing of a "public struggle" session. The scene may have been difficult for Kaige

to shoot because, as a former Red Guard himself, he had denounced his own father, the filmmaker Chen Huakai, at such a session, leading to Huakai's being sent to work at a rubber plantation for five years. "There was no human dignity at that time," Kaige admits. "Later I apologized to my father. Still, I cannot forgive myself." He did, however, make his father the film's production designer, whose job was to recreate Peking over a fifty-year span during the twenty-week shoot.

*Farewell, My Concubine*, with its keen insight into ambiguities of the head, heart, and loins, experienced one last irony. Submitted

by a proud China, it tied with another preconception-shaking love story for the Palme d'Or at Cannes, Jane Campion's story of a deaf feminist in *The Piano* (1993). After the magnifying glass of publicity, ostensibly due to a certain suicide in the film committed during Deng Xiaoping's glorious reform rule, the government later all but banned the screening of the film it had sponsored. Politics? Or perhaps the clench was due to a thornier issue? In Kaige's words, "What if a man can only realize his love for another man on the stage? What if he has no choice but to take theater as life itself?…I hope that people find this to be a story full of vitality and pleasing to

watch and that they don't subject it to the limitation of any set ideological viewpoint." May the same be said of every great movie love story happily, unhappily, or better yet realistically ever after.

*OPPOSITE: Newly divorced Vivian (Helen Shaver, at left) may not know it yet, but Vegas waitress Cay (Patricia Charbonneau) will reroute more than her travel plans in Desert Hearts (1985).*
*ABOVE: New housemate Marijo (Josiane Balasko) would like to keep the peace between Loli (Victoria Abril) and her philandering husband Laurent (Alain Chabat) but she's having too much fun sleeping with her and not with him in French Twist (1995).*

# ALL YOU NEED IS...

*It's a many splendored thing, a machine, a bug, and occasionally a gun. It's crazy, and happy, when on the run. It hurts,*
*especially at first bite, and it streams, especially in the afternoon, with a proper stranger. It leads the way,*
*finds Andy Hardy, and then laughs at Andy Hardy. It's better than ever, at the top, except when it kills. What is it?*
*From the mouths of movie stars through Hollywood history we may find our ultimate answer.*

## LINES

1. *Why must you bring in wrong values? Love is a roman-tic designation for a most ordinary biological, or shall we say chemical, process, and chemically we are quite sympathetic.*

2. *Maybe love is like luck. You have to go all the way to find it.*

3. *Don't you love me? / That's the tough part of it. But it'll pass. These things do in time.*

4. *If you had the choice would you rather love a girl or have her love you?*

5. *I don't want to be worshiped. I want to be loved.*

6. *Love is too weak a word for what I feel. I lurve you. I luff you.*

7. *You hit hard, baby, so you love hard.*

8. *I love you. I've loved you since the first moment I saw you. I guess maybe I even loved you before I saw you.*

9. *True love is erection, not orgasm.*

10. *The truth is, Charlie, you just don't care about anything except you. You just want to convince people that you love them so much that they should love you back.*

11. *Love! That's soft stuff. You move and it's suicide for both of you.*

12. *No one has ever loved you as I love you. / That may be true but what can I do about it?*

13. *My love has lasted longer than the temples of your gods. No man ever suffered as I did for you.*

14. *To the party of the first part—I love you. The party of the second part.*

15. *I'm in love with you and I want to marry you. / I'm in love with you and I want to marry you! / That cuts down on our love scenes quite a bit, doesn't it?*

16. *I love him because he's the kind of guy who gets drunk on a glass of buttermilk, and I love the way he blushes right up over his ears. I love him because he doesn't know how to kiss—the jerk!*

17. *I have loved you since the beginning of time. / But you only met me yesterday. / That was when time began.*

18. *You just stay away from me. / Edie, I—Edie, you love me. / I didn't say I didn't love you. I said stay away from me.*

19. *Just say you love me. You don't have to mean it.*

20. *Love means never having to say you're ugly.*

21. *When you love someone you go deaf, dumb, and blind.*

22. *I love a man I no longer love, so I try to love him more.*

23. *I don't think we don't love each other.*

24. *Makin' love is like hittin' a baseball. You just gotta relax and concentrate.*

25. *Would you still love me if I had little tits and worked in a fish house?*

26. *If love is blind, marriage is like having a stroke.*

## ACTOR & MOVIE

**A:** *Barbara Stanwyck in* Ball of Fire *(1941)*

**B:** *Woody Allen in* Annie Hall *(1977)*

**C:** *Clark Gable in* Strange Cargo *(1940)*

**D:** *Montgomery Clift in* A Place in the Sun *(1951)*

**E:** *Alain Cuny in* Emanuelle *(1974)*

**F:** *Edward G. Robinson in* Little Caesar *(1930)*

**G:** *Robert Taylor and Greta Garbo in* Camille *(1937)*

**H:** *Carolyn Jones in* The Bachelor Party *(1957)*

**I:** *Lizabeth Scott and Humphrey Bogart in* The Maltese Falcon *(1941)*

**J:** *Boris Karloff in* The Mummy *(1932)*

**K:** *Jimmy Stewart in* Made for Each Other *(1939)*

**L:** *Joseph Cotten in* Citizen Kane *(1941)*

**M:** *Lolita Davidovich in* Blaze *(1989)*

**N:** *Errol Flynn and Mary Stuart in* Don Juan *(1949)*

**O:** *Joel McCrea and Laraine Day in* Foreign Correspondent *(1940)*

**P:** *Eva Marie Saint and Marlon Brando in* On the Waterfront *(1954)*

**Q:** *Vincent Price in* The Abominable Dr. Phibes *(1971)*

**R:** *Susan Sarandon in* Bull Durham *(1988)*

**S:** *Romy Schneider in* Clair de Femme *(1979)*

**T:** *Jack Nicholson in* Carnal Knowledge *(1971)*

**U:** *Greta Garbo in* Ninotchka *(1939)*

**V:** *Danny DeVito in* The War of the Roses *(1989)*

**W:** *Robert Redford in* The Way We Were *(1973)*

**X:** *Robert Mitchum in* Out of the Past *(1947)*

**Y:** *Katharine Hepburn in* The Philadelphia Story *(1940)*

**Z:** *Jeremy Irons in* Betrayal *(1983)*

# BIBLIOGRAPHY

Agan, Patrick. *Hoffman Vs. Hoffman*. London: Robert Hale, 1986.

Alexander, Jan, and Lotte Da. *Bad Girls of the Silver Screen*. New York: Carroll & Graf Publishers, Inc., 1989.

*The All Movie Guide*. CompuServe Online, 1991–1995.

Alvarez, A. "Scenes from an Actress's Life." *New York Times Magazine*, December 22, 1974.

Anger, Kenneth. *Hollywood Babylon*. New York: Simon & Schuster, 1975.

Ansen, David, Dierdre Nickerson, and Marcus Henry. "The Real Cultural Revolution." *Newsweek*, November 1, 1993.

Astaire, Fred. "The Role I Liked Best." *The Saturday Evening Post*, July 3, 1948.

——. *Steps in Time*. New York: Harper and Brothers Publishers, 1959.

Atwan, Robert, and Bruce Forer. *Bedside Hollywood: Great Scenes from Movie Memoirs*. New York: Moyer Bell Limited, 1985.

Austin, John. "Katharine Ross: I'm Afraid I Won't Stay Good." *Modern Movies*, August 1968.

Bach, Steven. *Marlene Dietrich: Life and Legend*. New York: William Morrow, 1992.

Bacon, James. "Tuesday Weld May Get Role of Lolita." *Los Angeles Mirror*, August 15, 1960.

Barrios, Gregg. "This Is 'Like Water' for Real." *Los Angeles Times*, October 17, 1994.

Bart, Peter. "Woolf at Hollywood's Door." *New York Times*, July 12, 1964.

Barth, Jack. "Spike Lee on Deck." *Village Voice*, August 12, 1996.

Belser, Lee. "Lolita Criticized, Well Defended." *Los Angeles Mirror*, April 10, 1961.

——. "Lolita Strewn Across Nation, Author Reveals." *Mirror News*, July 31, 1959.

Billen, Stephanie. "How to Cook Up a Storm." *London Times*, September 30, 1993.

Brando, Marlon, and Robert Lindsey. *Brando: Songs My Mother Taught Me*. New York: Random House, 1994.

Brasel, Dale. "Mad About Shue." *Detour*, November 1995.

Brennan, Judy. "Not Your Average Nymphet." *Los Angeles Times*, July 15, 1995.

*The Bridges of Madison County*–Warner Brothers publicity material.

Brown, Peter H. "The Art of the Love Scene." *Us*, May 14, 1990.

Bunzel, Peter. "Yes, They Did It: Lolita Is a Movie." *Life*, May 25, 1962.

Burkhart, Jeff, and Bruce Stuart. *Hollywood's First Choices*. New York: Crown Publishers, 1994.

Byron, Stuart. "Rules of the Game." *Village Voice*, September 25, 1981.

Cameron, Sue. "Arthur Hiller Tells How to Make a Hit: Love Story." *Hollywood Reporter*, July 12, 1971.

Canby, Vincent. "Screen: Prediction and a 'Love Story.'" *New York Times*, December 27, 1970.

Carey, Gary. Tribute to George Cukor–Museum of Modern Art Department of Film, October 1970.

Celebrity Gossip??

Champlin, Charles. "Bergman Looks at the Ties that Bind." *Los Angeles Times*, November 18, 1973.

——. "Sophia Gets the Bird." *Los Angeles Times*, October 27, 1977.

——. "This Is a Fine Romance." *Los Angeles Times*, July 27, 1996.

Chase, Donald. "'Moonstruck': Filming Crazy Love Stories." *Los Angeles Times*, March 1, 1987.

Christy, George. "The Great Life." *Hollywood Reporter*, July 1, 1993.

Ciment, Michael. *Kazan on Kazan*. New York: Viking Press, 1974.

Clark, Paul. "'The Graduate' Remains a Pop Icon." *Long Beach Telegram*, January 10, 1993.

Cohen, Joan L. The Rose Tattoo–Los Angeles County Museum of Art Film Series, August 31, 1974.

Coie, Peter. *Ingmar Bergman*. New York: Charles Scribner & Sons, 1982.

Corey, Melinda, and George Ochoa. *The Man in Lincoln's Nose*. New York: Simon & Schuster, 1990.

Corliss, Richard. "Torrid Movie, Hot New Star." *Time*, August 24, 1981.

Crain, Mary Beth. "Top Hat." *Los Angeles Weekly*, October 5, 1990.

Crawley, Tony. *The Films of Sophia Loren*. London: LSP Books, 1974.

Croce, Arlene. *The Fred Astaire and Ginger Rogers Book*. New York: Outerbridge and Lazard, Inc., 1972.

Dargis, Manhola. "Ring of Fire." *Los Angeles Weekly*, November 3, 1995.

De Rosso, Diane. *James Mason*. London: Lennard Publishing, 1989.

DeSimio, John. *The American President*–Castle Rock Entertainment publicity material.

Dewey, Donald. *Marcello Mastroianni: His Life and Art*. New York: Birch Lane Press, 1993.

Dolce, Joe. "Mississippi Masala." *Details*, March 1992.

Dutka, Elaine. "Sydney Pollack's Still Adapting." *Los Angeles Times*, July 18, 1993.

Ebert, Roger. "Actress Is Leaving Her Squeaky Clean Image Behind." *Sacramento Bee*, December 17, 1995.

——. "Interview with Nicolas Cage." The Ebert Co., Ltd.: November 1, 1995.

Eisner, Lotte H. *Murnau*. Los Angeles, Calif.: University of California Press, 1964.

Esimio, John. *When Harry Met Sally...*–Castle Rock Entertainment publicity material.

Eyman, Scott. *Ernst Lubitsch: Laughter in Paradise*. New York: Simon & Schuster, 1993.

*Farewell, My Concubine*–Montreal Film Festival publicity material.

Fishgall, Gary. *Against Type: The Biography of Burt Lancaster*. New York: Scribner and Sons, 1995.

Freedman, Samuel G. "One People in Two Worlds." *New York Times*, February 2, 1992.

Furth, George. "Katharine Ross: PostGraduate." *After Dark*, August 1969.

Gillespie, Dennis. "I Was an Extra in 'Love Story.'" *Glamour*, December 1970.

Glemis, Joseph. "Painful Therapy from John Cassavetes." *Newsday*, October 17, 1974.

Goldstein, Patrick. "A Jazzy Director Who's Got It." *Los Angeles Times*, August 25, 1986.

Goldstein, Toby. *William Hurt: the Man, the Actor*. New York: St. Martin's Press, 1987.

Gonzalez, Fernando. "A Tasty Transition to the Silver Screen for Chocolate." *Long Beach Press Telegram*, March 21, 1993.

Goodwin, Betty. "A Model of Simplicity." *Los Angeles Times*, June 1, 1995.

Gordon, Ruth. *My Side*. New York: Harper and Row, 1976.

Greenberg, Abe. "Pop Gun Injures Liz, Film Delayed." *Citizen News*, November 16, 1965.

——. "So Nobody's Afraid of Virginia Woolf!" *Citizen News*, October 20, 1965.

Hadleigh, Boze. *Hollywood Babble On*. New York: Birch Lane Press, 1994.

Hancock, Lynell. "A Place in the Heart." *Newsweek*, June 19, 1996.

Harmetz, Aljean. "Harold's Back and Maude's Got Him." *New York Times*, May 26, 1974.

Harris, Warren G. *Audrey Hepburn*. New York: Simon & Schuster, 1994.

Harvey, Stephen. *Directed by Vincent Minnelli*. New York: Harper & Row Publishers, 1989.

Harvith, Susan, and John Harvith. *Karl Struss: Man With a Camera*. The Los Angeles County Museum of Art: January 5, 1977.

Haun, Harry. *The Movie Quote Book*. New York: Lippincott & Crowell, 1980.

Herman, Jan. "Dalton Trumbo Asked Me to Front for Him." *Los Angeles Times*, August 25, 1991.

Higham, Charles. "The Family that Films Together May Win Oscars Together." *New York Times*, April 6, 1975.

Higham, Charles, and Hal Wallis. *Starmaker*. New York: Macmillan, 1980.

Higham, Charles, and Roy Mosely. *Cary Grant: The Lonely Heart*. New York: Harcourt, Brace & Jovanovich, 1989.

Hinson, Hal. "Meg Ryan: Coming of Age." *Time Out*, November 29–December 6, 1989.

Hoberman, J. "Beijing Opera Views." *Village Voice*, May 12, 1992.

Hockofler, Matile. *Marcello Mastroianni: The Fun of Cinema*. Rome: Gremese International, 1992.

"Hollywood-Nymphet Found." *Time*, October 10, 1960.

Hruska, Bronwen. "Making a Home for 'The Bridges of Madison County.'" *Us*, June 1995.

Jaccard, Roland. *Louise Brooks: Portrait of an Anti–Star*. New York: New York Zoetrope, 1986.

Jennings, Robert C. "All for the Love of Mike." *The Saturday Evening Post*, October 9, 1965.

Jivani, Alkarim. "Lust in Spice." *Time Out*, January 15–22, 1992.

Johnson, Grady. "Key West Playwright Gets into 'Tattoo' Act." *New York Times*, December 5, 1954.

Jordan, Richard. *Pretty Woman*–Touchstone Pictures publicity material.

Kanter, Stefan. "The Love Bug." *Time*, December 21, 1970.

Karney, Robyn. *Audrey Hepburn: A Star Danced*. New York: Arcae Publishing, 1995.

Katz, Ian. "'Vegas' Writer Lost His Fight." *Long Beach Press Telegram*, January 24, 1996.

Kazan, Elia. *A Life*. New York: Alfred A. Knopf, 1988.

Kent, Leticia. "A Boy of 20 and a Woman of 80." *New York Times*, April 4, 1971.

Kilday, Greg. "When Billy Met Rob." *Los Angeles Times*, July 16, 1989.

Knight, Vivien. *Trevor Howard: a Gentleman and a Player*. London: Muller, Blond & White, 1986.

Leaming, Barbara. *Katharine Hepburn*. New York: Crown Publishers, 1995.

*Leaving Las Vegas*–United Artists publicity material.

Lee, David. *The Films of Spike Lee: Five for Five*. New York: Stewart, Tabori & Chang, 1991.

Lenne, Gerard. *Sex on the Screen*. New York: St. Martin's Press, 1978.

Levitt, Shelley et al. "Heartland." *People*, June 26, 1995.

Levy, Emanuel. *George Cukor: Master of Elegance*. New York: William Morrow, 1994.

Lindsay, Cynthia. "Who's Afraid of Virginia Woolf." *Cue*, June 1965.

"Magnani in Hollywood." *Cue*, November 5, 1955.

Mankin, Eric. "The Ties that Bind." *Los Angeles Reader*, October 22, 1993.

Manso, Peter. *Brando*. New York: Hyperion, 1994.

Martin, Mick, and Marsha Porter. *Video Movie Guide 1995*. New York: Ballantine Books, 1995.

——. *Video Movie Guide 1996*. New York: Ballantine Books, 1996.

Matthews, Tom. "Norman Jewison Gets 'Moonstruck.'" *Box Office*, January 1988.

McClelland, Doug. *Star Speak*. Boston: Faber & Faber, 1987.

McDougal, Dennis. "Take Five." *Los Angeles Times*, October 22, 1989.

McGilligan, Patrick. *George Cukor: a Double Life*. New York: St. Martin's Press, 1991.

McGregor, Alex. "A Conference with the President." *Box Office*, November 1995.

McGuie, Ann. "Kate in Control." *American Movie Classics Magazine*, March 1993.

McKenna, Kristine. "Playing Cards as They're Dealt." *Los Angeles Times*, October 29, 1995.

Miller, Clive. Tribute to Katharine Hepburn–Los Angeles County Museum of Art, June 5, 1981.

Miner, Jan. "'Moonstruck' on Location in New York." *Back Stage*, January 23, 1987.

*Mississippi Masala*–Samuel Goldwyn Company publicity material.

Mitchell, Sean. "Clint by Candlelight." *Los Angeles Times Calendar*, May 28, 1995.

Moley, Raymond. *The Hays Office*. New York: Bobbs Merrill Company, 1945.

Mosley, Philip. *Ingmar Bergman: The Cinema as Mistress*. London: Marion Boyars, 1981.

"My Fair Lady." *TV Guide*, March 31, 1990.

Nabokov, Vladimir. *Lolita*. New York: Berkeley Publishing, 1955.

Newquist, Roy. "Behind the Scenes of a Shocking Movie." *McCalls*, June 1966.

Nickens, Christopher. *Natalie Wood: A Biography in Pictures*. Garden City, N.Y.: Dolphin Books, 1986.

Nowlan, Robert A., and Gwendolyn M. *Film Quotations*. Jefferson, N.C.: McFarland & Company, 1994.

Outerbridge, David. *Without Makeup: Liv Ulmann*. New York: William Morrow & Company, 1979.

Outlaw, Marpessa. "The Mira Stage." *Village Voice*, February 18, 1992.

*The Oxford Dictionary of Quotations*. 3rd ed. Oxford: The Oxford University Press, 1979.

Parish, James Robert. *The Paramount Pretties*. New Rochelle, N.Y.: Arlington House, 1972.

Patterson, Alex. *Spike Lee*. New York: Avon Books, 1992.

"The Philadelphia Story." *Look*, December 31, 1940.

Piagnesi, Patrizia. *Anna Magnani*. Milan: Fabbri Editori, 1988.

Pryor, Thomas. "By Way of Report." *New York Times*, February 9, 1941.

Puig, Claudia. "He's Up. He's Down. He's Up. He's Down. He's Up for Good?" *Los Angeles Times Magazine*, February 4, 1996.

"Red Spree." *New York Times*, October 13, 1957.

"Return Ticket." *London Times*, August 2, 1995.

Robertson, Patrick. *Guiness Film Facts and Feats*. Middlesex, England: Guiness Superlatives Limited, 1985.

Roderick, Kyle. *Married in the Movies*. San Francisco: Collins Publishers, 1994.

*Roman Holiday*–Denver Film Festival programme notes, July 1993.

Ruuth, Marianne. "New Hit Comedy Launches a Star: Meg Ryan." *Hello*, July 1989.

Ryan, James. "Brainy Siren, Now Mom." *New York Times*, November 12, 1995.

Saxon, Wolfgang. "Edgar Scott, 96, Investment Banker and Socialite." *New York Times*, May 30, 1995.

Schesler, Ken. *This is Hollywood*. Redlands, Calif.: Ken Schesler Publishing, 1995.

Scheuer, Philip K. "Hal Wallis Buys Another Southern Play by Williams." *Los Angeles Times*, December 12, 1954.

Schickel, Richard. *Brando: A Life in Our Times*. New York: Antheum, 1991.

——. "The Cowboy and the Lady." *Time*, June 5, 1995.

Schwartz, Cynthia. *Farewell, My Concubine*–Mirimax Films publicity material.

Scott, Vernon. "Minsky's Side of 'Love Story'." *Los Angeles Herald Examiner*, May 28, 1972.

"Sheet Music." *People*, April 6, 1992. Shevey, Sandra. "A Woman Out from Under the Influence." *New York Times*, March 7, 1975.

Shipman, David. *Movie Talk*. New York: St. Martin's Press, 1988.

Siegel, Jeff. *The Casablanca Companion*. Dallas: Taylor Publishing, 1992.

Siegel, Scott, and Barbara Siegel. *American Film Comedy*. New York: Prentice Hall, 1994.

Siegel, Scott, and Tamara Siegel. "United Artists' 'Leaving Las Vegas' Arrives." *Dramalogue*, October 26–November 1, 1995.

Silverman, Stephen M. *David Lean*. New York: Harry N. Abrams, Inc., 1989.

Sinclair, Marianne. *Hollywood Lolitas*. New York: Henry Holt and Co., 1988.

Spector, Warren. *Cinema Texas*–program notes. Vol. 22, No. 1, January 28, 1982.

Star, Michael. *Peter Sellers: A Film History*. Jefferson, N.C.: McFarland Publishers, 1991.

Stefoff, Rebecca. *Kathleen Turner: An Unauthorized Biography*. New York: St. Martin's Press, 1987.

Stoner, Tad. "Kaige Says 'Farewell' to Lone." *Hollywood Reporter*, January 7, 1992.

Suber, Howard. "Dalton Trumbo's Real Role in 'Roman Holiday.'" *Los Angeles Times*, August 19, 1991.

Sullivan, Ed. "The Reviewing Stand." *Hollywood Citizen*, December 2, 1940.

Swindell, Larry. *Body and Soul: The Story of John Garfield*. New York: William Morrow and Company, Inc., 1975.

"Talking with 'Love Story' Segal." *After Dark*, December 3, 1969.

Thomas, Bob. "Cary Grant Spurns Bid to Play Lead in Lolita." *Morrior News*, October 6, 1958.

Thomas, Kevin. "'Sunrise' Opens Karl Struss Film Series at L.A.C.M.A." *Los Angeles Times*, January 3, 1977.

Tims, Hilton. *Emotion Pictures*. London: Columbus Books, 1987.

Tolton, Cam. *The Rose Tattoo*–The Toronto Film Society, Programme 1, October 8, 1986.

Tonetti, Claretta Micheletti. *Benardo Bertolucci*. New York: Twayne Publishers, 1995.

The Toronto Film Society Silent Series. Programme 7, March 23, 1987.

Travers, Peter. "The Little Film that Could." *Us*, March 1996.

Turan, Kenneth. "A Top Year for Chinese Language Film." *Los Angeles Times*, May 24, 1993.

Valentino, Lou. *The Films of Lana Turner*. Secaucus, N.J.: Citadel Press, 1976.

Walker, Alexander. *Audrey: Her Real Story*. New York: St. Martin's Press, 1994.

———. *Dietrich*. Cambridge, Mass.: Harper and Row, 1984.

———. *Peter Sellers*. New York: MacMillan, 1981.

Warga, Wayne. "Why He's in 'Love Story.'" *Los Angeles Times*, March 28, 1971.

"Warner Brothers Exhib Pledge Not to Show Minors 'Woolf' Valenti's 1st Hot Potato?" *Variety*, May 26, 1964.

Weber, Bruce. "Can Men and Women Be Friends?" *New York Times*, July 9, 1989.

Wells, Jeffrey. "Geez, Just Because You Think It's a Good Story Doesn't Mean There's a Movie in It." *Los Angeles Times*, January 24, 1993.

Whitcomb, Jon. "Leslie Caron as 'Gigi'." *Cosmopolitan*, May 1958.

Willman, Chris. "Auteur! Auteur!" *Pulse*, November 1994.

Wines, Michael. "Hollywood Finds a Presidential Role Model." *New York Times*, November 12, 1995.

Zimmerman, Paul D. "Love Death and Tears." *Newsweek*, December 28, 1970.

Zimmerman, Paul. "Nick Vs. Mabel." *Newsweek*, December 9, 1974.

"Zuckor's Office as Harvard Deanery." *Variety*, December 17, 1969.

# PHOTOGRAPHY CREDITS

# INDEX